Lab Manual for MCTS Guide to Microsoft® Windows Server® 2008 Network Infrastructure Configuration (Exam #70-642)

Michael Bender

COURSE TECHNOLOGY
CENGAGE Learning™

Australia • Brazil • Japan • Korea • Mexico • Singapore • Spain • United Kingdom • United States

COURSE TECHNOLOGY
CENGAGE Learning™

**Lab Manual for MCTS Guide to Microsoft®
Windows Server® 2008 Network Infrastructure
Configuration (Exam # 70-642)**
Author: Michael Bender

Vice President, Career and Professional Editorial:
Dave Garza

Executive Editor: Stephen Helba

Acquisitions Editor: Nick Lombardi

Managing Editor: Marah Bellegarde

Senior Product Manager: Michelle Ruelos
Cannistraci

Editorial Assistant: Sarah Pickering

Vide President, Career and Professional Marketing:
Jennifer Ann Baker

Marketing Director: Deborah S. Yarnell

Senior Marketing Manager: Erin Coffin

Associate Marketing Manager: Shanna Gibbs

Production Director: Carolyn Miller

Production Manager: Andrew Crouth

Content Project Manager: Allyson Bozeth

Art Director: Jack Pendleton

Cover designer: Getty Images

Cover photo or illustration: Getty Images

Manufacturing Coordinator: Julio Esperas

Copyeditor: Kathy Orrino

Proofreader: Sarah Truax

Compositor: KnowledgeWorks Global Ltd.

For product information and technology assistance, contact us at
Cengage Learning Customer & Sales Support, 1-800-354-9706

For permission to use material from this text or product,
submit all requests online at **www.cengage.com/permissions.**
Further permissions questions can be e-mailed to
permissionrequest@cengage.com

Example: Microsoft ® is a registered trademark of the Microsoft Corporation.

Library of Congress Control Number: 2010921125

ISBN-13: 978-1-423-90274-4
ISBN-10: 1-423-90274-2

Course Technology
20 Channel Center Street
Boston, MA 02210
USA

Cengage Learning is a leading provider of customized learning solutions with office
locations around the globe, including Singapore, the United Kingdom, Australia,
Mexico, Brazil, and Japan. Locate your local office at: **international.cengage.com/
region**

Cengage Learning products are represented in Canada by
Nelson Education, Ltd.

For your lifelong learning solutions, visit **course.cengage.com**
Visit our corporate website at **cengage.com**.

Printed in the United States of America
1 2 3 4 5 6 7 12 11 10

Contents

Introduction

The objective of this lab manual is to provide you with hands-on activities that will help prepare you for the Microsoft Certified Technology Specialist (MCTS) exam #70-642: Windows Server 2008 Network Infrastructure–Configuring. This manual is intended to be used along with the Course Technology book *MCTS Guide to Microsoft Windows Server 2008 Network Infrastructure Configuration*.

The activities in this book can be completed by students within a classroom or through individual study with access to the proper equipment. For the optimal hands-on experience, students will complete the activities in the main textbook as well as the activities in this lab manual. However, these labs were designed to be completed apart from the activities in the textbook, so students can complete the activities in the textbook in one environment and the activities in this manual in a different environment if desired.

Ideally, these labs will be performed in a virtual machine environment so that students do not require multiple sets of computer hardware or lab partners. However, there is no reason the labs cannot be completed using multiple physical computers connected to a LAN. The labs are written with the assumption that a single student will complete all of the steps in an activity.

Features

This lab manual includes the following features to provide a successful learning experience:

- Lab Objectives—The learning objectives of each lab are stated at the beginning of each activity.

- Materials Required—Every lab includes information on the hardware and software needed to complete the lab.

- Estimated Completion Time—Every lab contains an estimated completion time, to help students organize their lab time effectively.

- Activity Background—Activity Background information provides important details for each lab and places the lab activity within the context of the learning objectives.

- Activity Sections—Labs are presented in manageable sections and include figures to reinforce learning.

- Step-by-Step Instructions—When a particular task is presented for the first time, step-by-step instructions are provided to complete the activity. However, if a task has already been presented in an earlier lab, the provided instructions are usually more generalized.

- Certification Exam Objectives—For each chapter, the relevant exam objectives are listed.

- Review Questions—Review questions that reinforce a student's understanding of the completed activity are provided for each lab.

Computer Requirements

A minimum of two computers are required. These can be virtual machines or physical computers. Each machine has the following minimum requirements:

Component	Requirement
CPU	Minimum: 1 GHz for x86 CPU or 1.4 GHz for x64 CPU
Memory	Minimum: 512 MB RAM for Windows Server 2008 installations and 1 GB RAM for Vista
Drives	Hard drive with at least 30 GB unallocated to install Windows Server 2008 or Vista One additional unallocated hard drive DVD-ROM drive
Networking	Network interface card with connection to the Internet A switch or hub is necessary if using physical computers.
Display and peripherals	Super VGA or higher Keyboard and mouse

Host System Requirements (when using virtualization)

The following table lists the hardware requirements for the host workstation when virtualization is used. Specific requirements for the chosen virtualization software may vary. Please see the Appendix for virtualization software options in the textbook, *MCTS Guide to Microsoft Windows Server 2008 Network Infrastructure Configuration* (ISBN: 142390236X).

Operating System	Suitable operating system to run the chosen virtualization software
CPU	Pentium 4 1.8 GHz minimum; Dual-core CPU of at least 1.6 GHz recommended CPU requirements will vary depending upon the virtualization software used.
Memory	2 GB RAM minimum
Drives	Hard drive with at least 50 GB free One additional unallocated hard drive DVD-ROM drive
Networking	Network interface card with connection to the Internet
Display and peripheral	SVGA or better monitor; bigger is preferred for working with multiple virtual machines; dual monitors are ideal but not necessary Keyboard and mouse

Software Requirements

- Windows Server 2008, Enterprise Edition
- Windows Automated Installation Kit for Windows Server 2008
- Microsoft Baseline Security Analyzer 2.1.1. or greater

Lab Setup

Successful completion of all labs requires three different Windows Server 2008 installations (two full installations and one Server Core installation) and one Windows Vista installation (or Windows XP or Windows 7). See the following table for the recommended naming conventions and IP addressing of each server, and how each server is used:

Installation	Name	IP Address	Usage
Windows Server 2008 Full Installation	LABSRVXX	• Internet-accessible address • 192.168.1.201 • Subnet mask: 255.255.255.0	Primary server used in most labs. Domain controller for domain netlab.local. Requires a network adapter that has access to the Internet or public network such as your school/lab network.
Windows Server 2008 Full Installation	LABSRV1XX	• 192.168.1.203 • Subnet mask: 255.255.255.0	Used in Chapters 9–11 as a second server. There is no activity for building this server; students should build the server using a basic install of Windows Server 2008.
Windows Server 2008 Server Core	LABSCXX	• 192.168.1.202 • Subnet mask: 255.255.255.0	Used in Chapters 5–11 to perform administrative tasks on a Server Core machine.

Note: Various lab activities in this manual will require access to Internet resources. If the given IP addressing scheme does not work in your network environment, you can come up with your own, ensuring that no two computers running at the same time share the same address.

A maximum of two operating systems are required to run at any one time, but when two OSs are running at the same time, one of them will always be LABSRVXX. If students are using virtualization, each operating system can reside in its own virtual machine which can be started as necessary. If students are using two or more physical computers, a multi-boot environment can be used. For example, if two physical computers are used, LABSRVXX can be installed on one physical computer and LABSCXX and LABSRV1XX can be installed on separate partitions of the second computer.

The first chapter instructs students to install Windows Server 2008 on one of their lab computers or virtual machines. In Chapter 2, students will be instructed to install Windows Server 2008 Server Core. The installation of the second Windows Server 2008 installation is not covered in the lab activities but the server will need to be available starting in Chapter 9.

CHAPTER ONE

INTRODUCTION TO WINDOWS SERVER 2008

Labs included in this chapter

- Lab 1.1 Installing and Configuring Windows Server 2008, Enterprise Edition
- Lab 1.2 Researching Microsoft Certifications and Exams
- Lab 1.3 Identifying Roles and Features in Windows Server 2008
- Lab 1.4 Installing Windows Server 2008 Roles and Features
- Lab 1.5 Working with Windows PowerShell

Lab 1.1 Installing and Configuring Windows Server 2008, Enterprise Edition

Objectives

The object of this activity is to install and configure a working version of Windows Server 2008 for use in subsequent lab activities.

 Depending on your lab environment, you may or may not need to complete this activity. Please check with your instructor before proceeding with this activity.

Materials Required

This lab requires the following:

- Physical computer or virtual machine that meets the minimum requirements for installation of Windows Server 2008.

Estimated completion time: **40–70 minutes** (depending on hardware configuration of lab environment)

Activity Background

Thanks to improvements in the installation and configuration processes, Windows Server 2008 installs more quickly and easily than previous versions of Windows Server. The initial install process uses Windows PE to collect system information and install the operating system files. After this is complete, the system begins the Out-of-Box Experience (OOBE), in which administrators perform the initial configuration of the server including name, networking information, and date/time settings. Upon completion of these two phases, the server is ready to join other computers on the network.

 Throughout the activities, your instructor might give you additional steps to perform, depending on your lab environment. All the activities in this chapter are appropriate for physical machines and virtual machine applications.

Activity

1. Place your Windows Server 2008 DVD in the DVD drive of your computer and then restart or power on your computer.

2. If prompted by the startup screen, press any key to boot from the DVD. You are prompted only if the computer has an existing operating system. The first part of the installation program starts.

3. When the first Install Windows window appears, confirm your time and currency format and that the keyboard layout is correct, and then click **Next**. The next Install Windows window appears, prompting you to start the installation, as shown in Figure 1-1.

4. Click **Install Now**. The Type your product key for activation window is displayed.

5. Enter your product key if you have one and are required to enter the key. You might be able to install Windows Server 2008 without a product key.

 Depending on the type of installation media and license model you are using, you may not be prompted for a product key. If this is the case, skip to Step 7.

Figure 1-1   Install Windows window

6. Click the **Automatically activate Windows when I'm online** check box to remove the check mark and then click **Next**. If you did not enter a product key, a message appears asking whether you want to enter a key. Click **No** to continue installing without a product key.

7. In the next window, select the version of Windows Server 2008 you will be installing. For this activity, choose **Windows Server 2008 Enterprise (Full Installation)** and then check the **I have selected the edition of Windows that I purchased** box, as shown in Figure 1-2. Click **Next**.

Figure 1-2   Selecting the version of Windows Server 2008 for installation

8. In the next window, read the Microsoft Software License Terms, check the **I accept the license terms** check box, and then click **Next**.

9. In the next window, click **Custom** to perform a custom installation, which is the appropriate option for performing a new installation. Notice that the choice to upgrade is not available. (Chapter 2 covers upgrading Windows Server 2008.)

10. If necessary, delete any existing partitions by completing the following steps in the **Where do you want to install Windows?** window:

   a. Click the partition you want to delete.

   b. Click the **Drive options (advanced)** link to display partitioning options.

   c. Click **Delete**.

   d. Click **OK** to confirm you want to delete the partition and lose all its data.

11. Click **Disk 0 Unallocated Space** and then click **Drive options (advanced)** to perform disk partitioning operations. Click **New**. Enter **30000** in the Size text box and ensure that this still leaves you with at least 10 GB of unallocated disk space. Click **Apply**.

12. Select **Disk 0 Partition 1** and then click **Format**. Confirm that you understand that all data will be lost when you format the partition by clicking **OK**. Click **Next**. Windows performs a number of tasks that do not require your input. This portion of the installation takes approximately 30 minutes depending on the hardware setup of your lab computer. The system will reboot one or more times during the installation. If you are prompted to press a key to start from DVD, ignore the message.

13. When advised that you need to change your password before logging on for the first time, click **OK**. Use **P@ssw0rd** as your new password. Enter the password twice to ensure it is correct and then click the arrow to submit the new password. When prompted that your password has changed, click **OK**. Windows Server 2008 starts for the first time, checks for and applies any updates, and then displays the Initial Configuration Tasks window as shown in Figure 1-3. It will be displayed at log on until you complete all the tasks necessary and uncheck the Do not show this window at log on box.

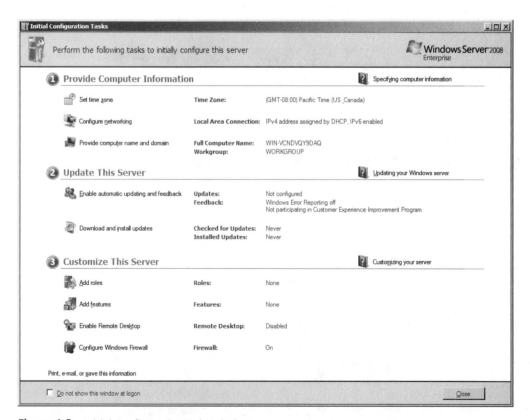

Figure 1-3   Initial Configuration Tasks window

14. In the Initial Configuration Tasks window, click **Set time zone**. The Date and Time dialog box opens. Click **Change time zone**, select your time zone in the Time zone drop-down list, and then click **OK**. If the date and time are incorrect, click **Change date and time**, change the time to your local time, and then click **OK**. Click **OK** to accept the changes and close the Date and Time dialog box.

 Ask your instructor if you are not sure of the proper time zone for your location.

15. In the Initial Configuration Tasks window, click **Provide computer name and domain**. The System Properties dialog box opens.

16. On the Computer Name tab, click **Change**. The Computer Name/Domain Changes dialog box opens.

17. Replace the current computer name with **LABSRVXX**, where XX is a number supplied by your instructor. Your number should be unique so each student has a different server name.

18. Click **OK** to accept the new name. A message box appears, informing you that a restart is needed. Click **OK** to close the message box.

19. Click **Close** to close the System Properties dialog box. When a Microsoft Windows dialog box appears, click **Restart Now** to restart your system.

20. After your system restarts, log on by pressing **Ctrl+Alt+Del**. Enter **P@ssw0rd** as your password and then press **Enter**.

21. When the Initial Tasks Configuration window opens, click the **Do not show this window at log on** check box.

22. Log off your server.

Review Questions

1. Which of the following editions of Windows Server 2008 is not available from the Windows Server 2008 installation media?

    a. Windows Server 2008 Standard

    b. Windows Server 2008 Web

    c. Windows Server 2008 Enterprise

    d. Windows Server 2008 Datacenter

2. Which of the following can be configured during the initial installation phase for Windows Server 2008?

    a. Time and date information

    b. Administrator password

    c. Licensing key

    d. Computer name

3. In addition to installing Windows Server 2008, what additional tasks can be performed using the installation media?

    a. Partition a hard drive

    b. Check system memory

    c. Perform a system restore

    d. All of the above

4. True or False? Windows Server 2008 can be installed without choosing the edition.

5. The process in which you perform the initial configuration of a Windows Server 2008 installation is called the _____ or _____.

Lab 1.2 Researching Microsoft Certifications and Exams

Objectives

The objective of this activity is to learn more about the Microsoft Certified Information Technology Professional (MCITP) – Server Administrator certification, and the MCTS Exam 70-642: Windows Server 2008 Network Infrastructure, Configuring.

Materials Required

This lab requires the following:

- A computer with Internet access

Estimated completion time: **15 minutes**

Activity Background

With the introduction of Windows Server 2008, Microsoft is introducing a new certification path for Server administrators called Microsoft Certified Information Technology Professional – Server Administrator, or MCITP – Server Administrator. This is a multiple-exam certification that will certify that a candidate has the knowledge to configure Windows Server 2008 networks. One of the exams for this certification is covered by this lab manual and the associated textbook. It is the **Microsoft Certified Technical Specialist (MCTS) Exam 70-642: Windows Server 2008 Network Infrastructure, Configuring** certification exam.

Activity:

1. Open your Web browser and go to **www.microsoft.com/learning**.
2. Search the Microsoft Learning Web site for **70-642**.
.3. In the search results, click the link for **TS: Windows Server 2008 Network Infrastructure, Configuring**.
4. On the Overview tab, click the link for **Microsoft Certified IT Professional (MCITP): Server Administrator** and review all the information on the resulting Web page.
5. Return to the exam Web page and review each of the tabs including **Overview, Skills Measured, Preparation Materials**, and **Community**.
6. Close your Web browser when you have completed reviewing the materials.

 It is not unusual for Web sites to change the location of where files are stored. If the URL above no longer functions, then open a search engine like Bing and search for "MCITP 70-642".

Review Questions

1. How many exams are required to receive the designation of MCITP – Server Administrator?

   a. 2

   b. 3

   c. 5

   d. 6

2. Which major topic has the greatest weight percentage for the 70-642 exam?

   a. Configuring IP Addressing and Services

   b. Configuring Name Resolution

c. Configuring Network Access

d. Configuring File and Print Services

e. Monitoring and Managing a Network Infrastructure

3. Which of the following exams is not required for the MCITP – Server Administrator certification?

a. Exam 70-640

b. Exam 70-642

c. Exam 70-643

d. Exam 70-646

4. The MCITP – Server Administrator certification replaces the _____ and _____ Windows Server 2003 certifications.

5. True or False? In order to take the 70-642 exam, you are required to have at least one year of verifiable experience implementing and administering a network operating system.

Lab 1.3 Identifying Roles and Features in Windows Server 2008

Objectives

The objective of this activity is to identify features and roles available in Windows Server 2008, and to become familiar with the Servermanagercmd.exe installation commands for each.

Materials Required

This lab requires the following:

- Physical computer or virtual machine running Windows Server 2008
- A pencil or pen

Estimated completion time: **15 minutes**

Activity Background

In Chapter 1, you learned about roles and features in Windows Server 2008. By adding roles, administrators give specific job responsibilities to a Windows Server 2008 computer. Features, on the other hand, are specific duties a Windows Server 2008 computer will perform. Some features are subsets of larger roles, while others perform stand-alone duties.

Servermanagercmd.exe is a new option in Windows Server 2008. It allows administrators to install roles and features from the command prompt. This is helpful in cases where scripts are used for installation.

Activity

1. Log on to the Windows Server 2008 computer.

2. If Server Manager does not appear, open it from the Start menu.

3. In Server Manager, highlight **Roles** and click **Add Roles** to launch the Add Roles Wizard. This allows you to view all of the available roles and see descriptions of each.

4. Click **Next** in the Before you Begin window.

5. Review each of the roles listed in the Select Server Roles window.

6. Click **Cancel** and **Yes** when finished with your review to close the wizard.

7. Highlight **Features** and click **Add Features** to launch the Add Features Wizard. This will allow you to view all of the available features and see descriptions of each.

8. Review each of the features in the Select Server Features window.

Table 1-1   Identify and describe the Windows Server 2008 roles and features

	Role or Feature	Description
Windows Backup		
Remote Server Administration Tools		
Active Directory Domain Services		
DNS Server		
Windows PowerShell		
Windows Hyper-V		
DHCP		
WINS		

9. Click **Cancel** and **Yes** when completed with your review to close the wizard.

10. Complete Table 1-1 using the information available in the Add Roles and Add Features wizards.

11. When complete, log off your computer.

Review Questions

1. Which of the following is not a Windows Server 2008 role?

   a. DNS

   b. DHCP

   c. WINS

   d. NAP

2. How many roles are available in Windows Server 2008, Standard Edition on the 32-bit platform?

   a. 15

   b. 16

   c. 17

   d. 18

3. You are a consultant for a small company, Badger Industries. The company needs to provide the following services to their end users and network clients from a newly deployed Windows Server 2008 server:

   • Access to Accounting documents stored on a central server

   • Automatic assignment of IP addresses to network computers that do not use static IP addresses

   • The ability to remotely administer other Windows Server 2008 computers

   Based on the requirements above, what roles and/or features need to be installed on the new server? (Choose all that apply.)

   a. DNS

   b. DHCP

   c. File Services

   d. Power Shell

   e. Remote Server Administration Tools

   f. WINS

   g. File Sharing

4. Roles and Features can be added and managed through the _____ console.

5. True or False? Servermanagercmd.exe will install roles and features on both the Full version and Server Core version of Windows Server 2008.

Lab 1.4 Installing Windows Server 2008 Roles and Features

Objectives

The objective of this activity is to install roles and features on a Windows Server 2008 system.

Materials Required

This lab requires the following:

- The physical computer or virtual machine running Windows Server 2008, Enterprise (Full Edition) that was previously configured as LABSRVXX, or another name specified by your instructor.

Estimated completion time: **20–30 minutes**

Activity Background

It is much easier to install roles and features in Windows Server 2008 than it was in the previous version of Windows Server. This is due to the addition of the Server Manager console along with Servermanagercmd.exe. Server Manager is a centralized console providing access to all the necessary management tools in Windows Server 2008. Servermanagercmd.exe provides commands for installing roles and services from the command prompt. In this activity, you will be using both tools to install various roles and features. Some of these roles and features will be used in future activities and others will just be installed for practice using Server Manager and Servermanagercmd.exe.

Activity

1. Log on to the Windows Server 2008 server.
2. If the Server Manager console does not open, open it by clicking **Server Manager** from the pinned programs area in the Start menu.
3. In Server Manager, click the **Roles** section.
4. In the Preview Pane, click **Add Roles**. This launches the Add Roles wizard.
5. In the Before You Begin window, review the information and then click **Next**.
6. Click the **File Services** role and then click **Next** twice. Click **Next** again to install the default file server role service and do not add any role services at this time. Click **Install** to complete the installation of this role.
7. Click **Close** when the File Services role is installed.
8. In the left pane of the Server Manager console, click **Features** and then click **Add Features** in the right pane. The Add Features Wizard starts.
9. If the Before You Begin window appears, review the information and then click **Next**.
10. Click the **Windows PowerShell** feature listed and then click **Next** to review the features being installed on the next screen.
11. Click **Install** to install this feature. Click **Close** when the Windows PowerShell feature is installed.
12. Click **Start** and then type **cmd** in the Start Search text box.
13. In the list of search results, click **Cmd.exe** to open a Command Prompt window.
14. Type the following commands, pressing **Enter** after each one, to install the Windows Deployment Service role and the Remote Server Administration tools for Roles and Features, as shown in Figure 1-4:

    ```
    ServerManagerCmd.exe -install WDS

    ServerManagerCmd.exe -install RSAT-Feature-Tools

    ServerManagerCmd.exe -install RSAT-Role-Tools
    ```

15. Type **shutdown -r -t 0** and press **Enter** to restart the server.

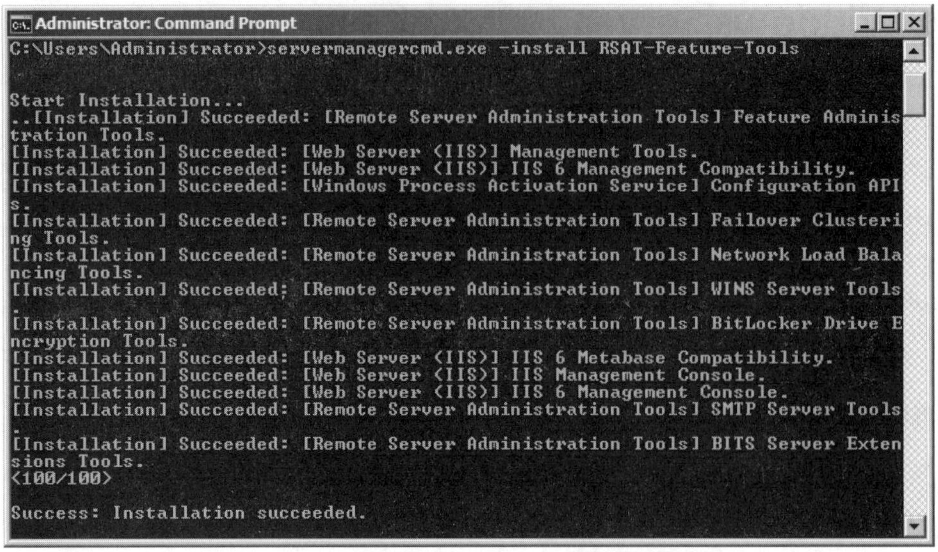

Figure 1-4 Running Servermanagercmd.exe from the command prompt

16. Log on to the Windows Server 2008 server.

17. Open the command prompt and execute the following command to verify the roles and features described above were installed:

    Servermanagercmd.exe -query

    All installed features and roles are highlighted in green in the command prompt.

18. Type **Exit** and then press **Enter** to close the Command Prompt window.

Review Questions

1. What is the correct syntax to uninstall the Distributed File System role service from Windows Server 2008?

    a. Servermanagercmd -uninstall DFS

    b. Servermanagercmd -uninstall FS-DFS

    c. Servermanagercmd -remove DFS

    d. Servermanagercmd -remove FS-DFS

    e. Servermanagercmd -delete DFS

    f. Servermanagercmd -delete DFS-FS

2. What color (by default) are installed roles and features when displayed through Servermanagercmd?

    a. Blue

    b. Green

    c. Black

    d. White

3. Which role service helps to protect networks, both public and private, from malware such as viruses and spyware?

    a. Network Access Protection

    b. Server Core

    c. Windows Firewall

    d. PowerShell

4. True or False? Servermanagercmd.exe will allow you to install multiple roles using a single command.

5. Servermanagercmd _____ will display all of the installed roles and features in Windows Server 2008.

Lab 1.5 Working with Windows PowerShell

Objectives

The objective of this lab is to perform common administrative tasks using Windows PowerShell.

Materials Required:

This lab requires the following:

- The physical computer or virtual machine running Windows Server 2008, Enterprise (Full Edition) that was previously configured as LABSRVXX, or another name specified by your instructor.

Estimated completion time: **15–20 minutes**

Activity Background

PowerShell is a command-line interface (CLI) and scripting language available in Windows Server 2008. Administrators can use PowerShell to perform various administrative and management tasks through the use of built-in commands called cmdlets. Cmdlets perform specific functions within the OS and follow a <noun>-<verb> naming syntax such as get-process. The results of PowerShell cmdlets can be used by other cmdlets as input through the process of pipelining.

In this lab, you use Windows PowerShell to perform basic administrative and management tasks. You will be introduced to the PowerShell command-line interface, which can be used to execute PowerShell tasks, and can be used in place of the traditional Windows command prompt for tasks such as nslookup, ping, and net.exe.

Activity

1. Log on to the Windows Server 2008 server.

2. Click **Start** and then type **PowerShell** in the Start Search text box.

3. In the list of search results, click **PowerShell 1.0** to open the PowerShell window.

4. Type **get-help** and press **Enter**. As shown in Figure 1-5, this displays information about the cmdlet along with helpful commands related to other PowerShell cmdlets.

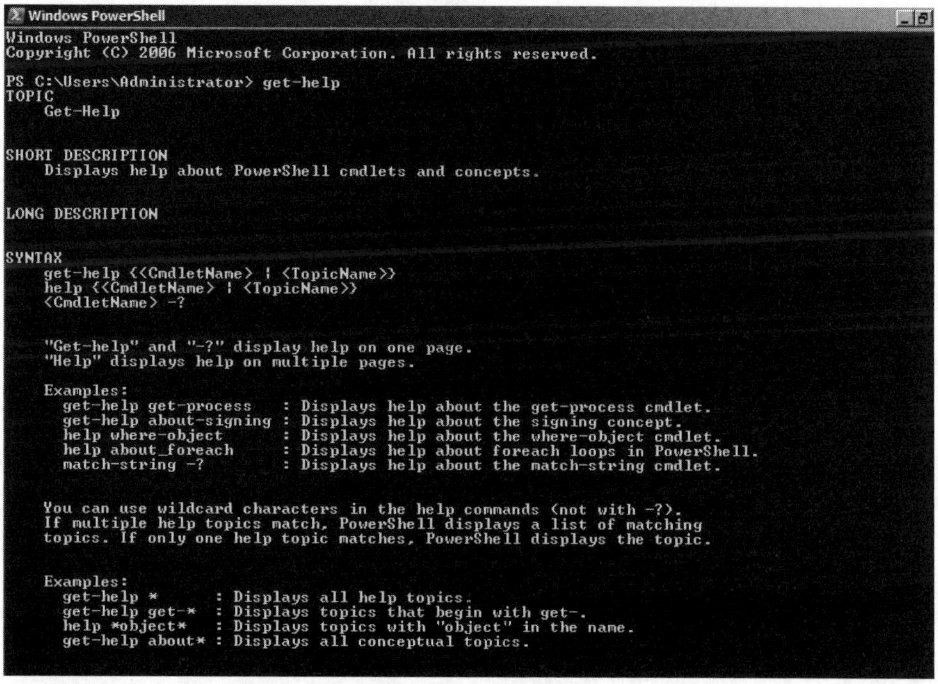

Figure 1-5 PowerShell window displaying get-help cmdlet

5. Type **get-command | format-table -wrap** and press **Enter** to display all of the PowerShell cmdlets by name and definition, including syntax. The "|", or pipe, is used to send output of one cmdlet into another cmdlet, which is called "pipelining."

6. Type **get-process** and press **Enter** to return a listing of all of the processes running on the server.

7. Type **get-help get-process** and press **Enter** to display help for the get-process cmdlet.

8. Type **get-help get-process -examples** and press **Enter** to view examples of the get-process cmdlet.

9. Type **get-help format-table -full** and press **Enter** to display the full help file for the format-table cmdlet including examples. The format-table cmdlet is used to define a format for cmdlet output.

10. Type **get-process | format-table -view priority** and press **Enter** to format the output of the get-process cmdlet in a table view that is sorted by priority.

11. Type **get-alias** and press **Enter** to list the current aliases available in PowerShell. PowerShell has built in aliases for cmdlets as well as the ability to create custom aliases.

12. Type **get-alias m*** and press **Enter** to list all of the aliases beginning with the letter "m."

13. Type **get-alias > alias.txt** and press **Enter** to send the results of the get-alias cmdlet to a text file.

14. Type **notepad alias.txt** and press **Enter** to open the alias.txt file in Notepad so you can view the output, which should look similar to Figure 1-6.

15. Type **get-history | format-list** and press **Enter** to format the cmdlet history using the format-list type.

16. Type **cls** and press **Enter** to clear the PowerShell window and place the prompt on the first line.

17. Type **nslookup microsoft.com** and press **Enter** to display the DNS host records for Microsoft. This is an example of using one of the many Windows command prompt commands within PowerShell.

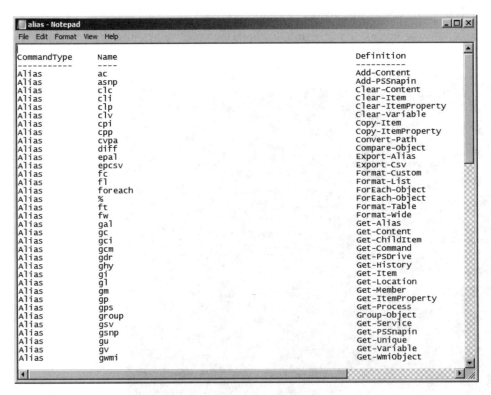

Figure 1-6 Results of get-alias command viewed in Notepad

Review Questions

1. Which of the following commands will not display information, including examples, about the suspend-service cmdlet?

    a. get-help suspend-service -details

    b. get-help suspend-service -examples

    c. get-help suspend-service -full

    d. get-help suspend-service –detailed

2. Which Microsoft product was the first to utilize Windows PowerShell?

    a. Windows XP, SP3

    b. Windows Server 2008

    c. Microsoft Exchange 2007

    d. Microsoft Office 2007

3. Which of the following switches can be used in place of get-help to display information on a cmdlet?

    a. -?

    b. -Help

    c. /?

    d. ?

4. _____ is the process of sending the output of one cmdlet into another cmdlet

5. True or False? PowerShell cmdlets can be run from either the PowerShell CLI or the Windows Command Prompt CLI.

INSTALLING WINDOWS SERVER 2008

Labs included in this chapter

- Lab 2.1 Installing the Windows Automated Installation Kit
- Lab 2.2 Creating a Custom WinPE Image
- Lab 2.3 Creating and Deploying a Windows Server 2008 Image Using WinPE
- Lab 2.4 Using Windows System Image Manager to Create an Answer File for Unattended Installations

Lab 2.1 Installing the Windows Automated Installation Kit

Objectives

The objective of this lab is to install the Windows Automated Installation Kit (WAIK) for use in future labs, and learn to use the WAIK documentation.

Materials Required

This lab requires the following:

- The physical computer or virtual machine running Windows Server 2008, Enterprise (Full Edition) that was previously configured as LABSRVXX, or another name specified by your instructor.
- A copy of the Windows Automated Installation Kit. This is downloadable from Microsoft.com as an ISO image file. Ensure you download the version that is appropriate for your environment, either x86 or x64.

Activity Background

Prior to Windows Server 2008 and Windows Vista, administrators had only a few options for imaging utilities from Microsoft. That changes with the introduction of the Windows Automated Installation Kit, or WAIK. The WAIK provides a comprehensive set of GUI-based and CLI-based utilities for imaging and installing Windows Server 2008. Included in the installation are ImageX and PEImg, which are used extensively when working with Windows Server 2008 images.

Estimated completion time: **45 minutes**

Activity

1. Log on to the Windows Server 2008 server.
2. Place your Windows Automated Installation Kit DVD in the DVD drive of your server.
3. When the AutoPlay window appears, click **Run StartCD.exe**. If AutoPlay is not enabled, click **Start > Computer** and double-click the CD/DVD drive that has the WAIK media.
4. Click **Windows AIK Setup** from the Welcome to Windows Automated Installation Kit menu.
5. Click **Next** on the Welcome Screen.
6. Click the **I Agree** radio button and click **Next**.
7. Click **Next** to choose the default installation directory for WAIK.
8. Click **Next** to confirm installation settings and begin installation.
9. Click **Close** when the installation is complete.
10. Close the Welcome to Windows Automated Installation Kit menu.
11. Click **Start > All Programs > Microsoft Windows AIK** to verify that Windows PE Tools Command Prompt and Windows System Image Manager are available.
12. Click **Start > All Programs > Microsoft Windows AIK > Documentation > Windows Automated Installation Kit User's Guide** to open the WAIK Users Guide as shown in Figure 2-1.
13. On the **Contents** tab in the User Guide, expand the **Deployment tools technical reference** section and review the following sections:

    a. ImageX Technical Reference

    b. Sysprep Technical Reference

    c. Windows PE Technical Reference

14. Close the WAIK User Guide when you have completed your review and log off your server.

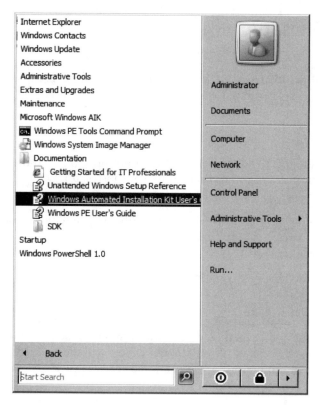

Figure 2-1   Opening the Windows Automated Installation Kit User's Guide

Review Questions

1. True or False? The Windows Automated Installation Kit is installed in Windows Server 2008 by default.

2. What interface provides the best access to the utilities installed with the WAIK?

    a. Windows PowerShell

    b. Windows RE Tools Command Prompt

    c. Windows PE Tools Command Prompt

    d. Windows Command Prompt

3. Which of the following is not installed as part of the Windows Automated Installation Kit?

    a. ImageX

    b. PEImg

    c. Sysprep

    d. Copype

4. Which of the following is not a switch for ImageX?

    a. /mount

    b. /apply

    c. /capture

    d. /details

5. _____ is a minimal Win32 operating system with limited services, built on the Windows Vista kernel.

Lab 2.2 Creating a Custom WinPE Image

Objectives

The objective of this lab is to create a custom Windows PE image for working with Windows Server 2008 images.

Materials Required

This lab requires the following:

- The physical computer or virtual machine running Windows Server 2008, Enterprise (Full Edition) that was previously configured as LABSRVXX, or another name specified by your instructor.
- Windows Server 2008 installation media or ISO image.
- An additional disk volume using the drive letter "E". Your instructor will provide you with instructions on setting up this disk volume if it does not exist.
- Installation of WAIK on LABSRVXX.

Activity Background

You have learned that Windows PE is the basis for the installation process for Windows Server 2008. In addition to installing the operating system, Windows PE can be used as part of the computer imaging process and for recovery tasks. Using tools from the Windows Automated Installation Kit, you will create a customized Windows PE image that you will be able to boot from to perform various administrative tasks.

Estimated completion time:	60 minutes

Activity

1. Log on to the Windows Server 2008 server.

2. Click **Start** > **All Programs** > **Microsoft Windows AIK** and select **Windows PE Tools Command Prompt**. This launches a custom command prompt for running the Windows PE tools needed for creating images, as shown in Figure 2-2.

3. Type **copype.cmd x86 e:\WinPeImg** and press **Enter**. This creates the directory structure needed to create a WinPE image in the e:\WinPeImg directory.

4. Type **dir** and press **Enter** to verify that the following directories are created:

   \WinPeImg\ISO

   \WinPeImg\mount

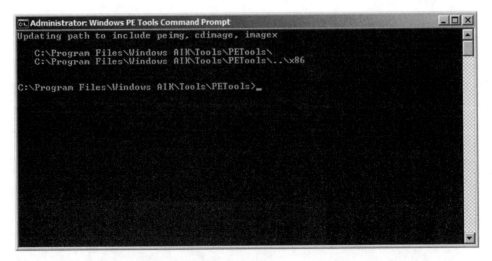

Figure 2-2 Windows PE Tools command prompt

5. Type `imagex /mountrw e:\WinPeImg\winpe.wim 1 e:\WinPeImg\mount` and press **Enter**. This mounts the WinPE .wim file to the \mount folder. The \mount folder contains all the files that will become part of your image and is where all additions are added.

6. To install additional packages into the Windows PE image, enter the following commands:

    `peimg /install=WinPE-HTA-Package e:\WinPeImg\mount\Windows`

    `peimg /install=WinPE-MDAC-Package e:\WinPeImg\mount\windows`

7. Type `peimg /list e:\WinPeImg\mount\Windows` and press **Enter**. This lists the packages available and the installation status.

8. Type `copy "c:\program files\Windows AIK\Tools\x86\imagex.exe" e:\WinPeImg\mount\windows` and press **Enter**. This copies imagex.exe to the \Windows directory, which results in it being loaded into memory during boot up and available from the command prompt.

9. Type `peimg /prep e:\WinPeImg\mount\Windows\`, press **Enter**, and type **Yes** when prompted. This prepares the image for use as shown in Figure 2-3.

10. Type `imagex /unmount Mount /commit` and press **Enter**. This commits all the changes that have been performed and unmounts the image files from ImageX.

11. Type `e:\WinPeImg\winpe.wim e:\WinPeImg\ISO\sources\boot.wim`, press **Enter**, and type **Yes**. This overwrites the default winpe.wim file with the updated winpe.wim file.

12. Type `oscdimg -n -be:\WinPeImg\etfsboot.com e:\WinPeImg\ISO e:\WinPeImg\WinPeImg.iso` and press **Enter**. This uses oscdimg to create an ISO image from your WinPE image files.

13. Browse to e:\WinPeImg\ and verify the WinPeImg.iso file is located in the directory.

14. Using a DVD-burning utility, create a bootable DVD of `e:\WinPeImg\WinPeImg.iso`. For virtual environments, copy the ISO file to a location where it can be mounted by your VM. This will most likely be the host machine.

Review Questions

1. What is the command to access an image file so the contents of the image can be modified?

    a. Imagex /mount -rw [imagefile] [imagenumber] [mountfolder]

    b. Imagex /write [imagefile] [imagenumber] [mountfolder]

    c. Imagex /mountrw [imagefile] [imagenumber] [mountfolder]

    d. Imagex /mount [imagefile] [imagenumber] [mountfolder]

2. Which of the following is a new command-line tool that can be used to capture, modify, and apply file-based disk images for rapid deployment?

    a. Oscdimg

    b. Copype

    c. Peimg

    d. ImageX

3. Which of the following is a new command-line tool for creating an .iso-based image file of a customized 32-bit or 64-bit version of Windows PE?

    a. Oscdimg

    b. Copype

    c. Peimg

    d. ImageX

4. True or False? ImageX cannot be used to create a full system backup of Windows Server 2008 for disaster recovery purposes.

5. _____ is a command-line tool for creating an image file (.iso) of a customized 32-bit or 64-bit version of Windows PE.

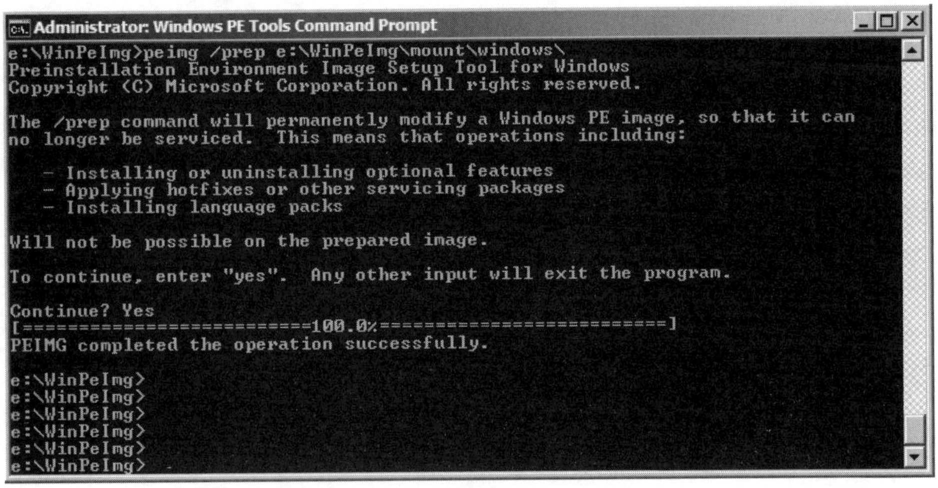

Figure 2-3   Preparing the Windows image with preimg /prep

Lab 2.3 Creating and Deploying a Windows Server 2008 Image Using WinPE

Objectives

The objective of this lab is to create and deploy a Windows Server 2008 image file using Windows PE.

Materials Required

This lab requires the following:

- The physical computer or virtual machine running Windows Server 2008, Enterprise (Full Edition) that was previously configured as LABSRVXX, or another name specified by your instructor.
- Windows Server 2008 installation media or ISO image
- An additional disk volume using the drive letter "E". Your instructor will provide you with instructions on setting up this disk volume if it does not exist.

Activity Background

The ability to create base images and deploy these images on your network is a necessary skill for any Windows administrator. As you have discovered, the manual installation process of Windows Server 2008 is fairly straightforward and efficient. However, even with the improved install process, there are many situations in which we need to deploy a customized installation of Windows Server 2008, or need to be able to distribute the image rapidly to a large install base. For such situations, administrators create image files. Image files, based on the Windows Image format (.wim), can be created and deployed with ImageX and the Windows Deployment Service. With ImageX, the easiest way to perform these tasks is through the use of a customized Windows PE installation containing the utility.

Estimated completion time: **90 minutes**

Activity

1. Boot the server from the WinPE DVD.
2. Press **any key** when the Press any key to boot from DVD message appears.
3. After a few minutes, you will be brought to the Windows PE command prompt as shown in Figure 2-4.

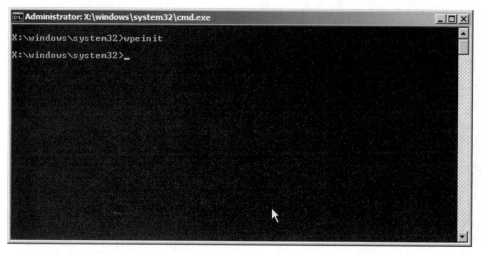

Figure 2-4 Windows PE command prompt

4. Type **imagex.exe /?** and press **Enter**. This verifies that imagex.exe is installed properly in your Windows PE image.

5. Type **d:** and press **Enter**. This should take you to the drive "E" that was available inside the OS.

6. Type **md 2008img** and press **Enter** to create a directory for storing your server image.

7. Type **x:** and press **Enter** to return to the default directory.

8. Type **imagex /compress maximum /capture c: d:\2008img\image.wim "Windows Server 2008 Image" /verify** and press **Enter**, as shown in Figure 2-5. This captures the image using maximum compression and verifies the image upon completion. Depending on the hardware setup of your server, this process may take from one to two hours to complete.

9. Type **dir d:** and press **Enter**. Verify that the file image.wim was created and is approximately 2-3 GB in size.

10. Type **x:** to return to the default directory.

11. Type **imagex /apply d:\2008img\image.wim 1 c:\ /verify** and press **Enter**. This applies the image you created previously to your server.

12. Type **exit** and press **Enter** to restart the machine and remove the DVD or ISO image from your computer.

13. Log on to LABSRVXX.

14. Open Server manager, if necessary.

15. Review the Server Manager summary and verify that the name of the server is LABSRVXX.

16. Log off the server.

Review Questions

1. By default, images created using ImageX are stored in what format?

   a. ISO

   b. IMG

   c. WIM

   d. WMI

2. Which of the following command switches can be used with ImageX?

   a. /capture

   b. /apply

   c. /shrink

   d. /compress

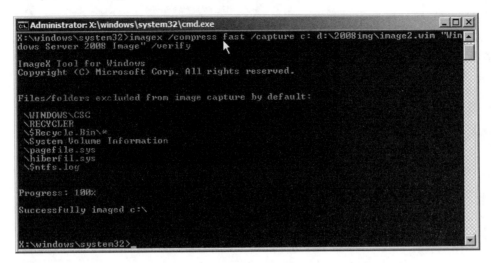

Figure 2-5   Capturing the Windows image with ImageX

3. Which of the following is not an option of the /compress switch?

   a. Fast

   b. Maximum

   c. Normal

   d. Slow

4. In order to work with an ImageX file it must be _____.

5. True or False? A deployable operating system image can be created using ImageX from within the GUI of Windows Server 2008.

Lab 2.4 Using Windows System Image Manager to Create an Answer File for Unattended Installations

Objectives
The goal of this lab is to create an answer file using WSIM for a Windows Server 2008 unattended installation.

Materials Required
This lab requires the following:

- The physical computer or virtual machine running Windows Server 2008, Enterprise (Full Edition) that was previously configured as LABSRVXX, or another name specified by your instructor.
- Windows Server 2008 installation media or ISO image
- An additional disk volume using the drive letter "E". Your instructor will provide you with instructions on setting up this disk volume if it does not exist.
- Installation of WAIK on LABSRVXX

Activity Background
One of the drawbacks of just using an image for OS installation is that administrators still need to perform some amount of manual configuration. That's where the Windows System Image Manager comes in. WSIM allows administrators to create answer files for automating the installation process. Answer files can provide install settings for all phases of the install process. These answer files are stored as .xml-based files that can be used by ImageX and other deployment tools such as Windows Deployment Services (WDS).

Estimated completion time: **25 minutes**

Activity

1. Log on to the Windows Server 2008 server.

2. Open a command prompt and type **xcopy d:*.* e:\W2K08Install\ /s** and press **Enter** to copy the Windows Server 2008 ISO files to a location on your server. Wait for the copy process to complete before moving to the next step.

3. Click **Start > All Programs > Microsoft Windows AIK** and select **Windows System Image Manager**. This console allows administrators to create and manage the imaging process.

4. In the Windows Image pane (in the bottom left corner), right-click **Select a Windows Image or catalog file**, and click **Select Windows Image**.

5. Select **e:\w2k08install\sources\install.wim** and click **Open**. This opens the Windows Server 2008 installation image file in WSIM, and allows you to choose which installation image you wish to work with.

6. Select **Windows Longhorn SERVERENTERPRISE** and click **OK**.

7. A message pops up indicating that the file is out of date. Click **Yes** to continue. WSIM begins generating a new catalog file as shown in Figure 2-6.

When WSIM is started for the first time, an Internet connection is required. WSIM will attempt to contact *http://crl.microsoft.com/pki/crl/products/CSPCA.crl* to get a PKIX-CRL Certificate Revocation List. If you do not have an Internet connection, you will receive a WSIM error message that reads "Windows System Image Manager execution failed. Details: Parameter count mismatch and WSIM will close."

8. Click **File, New Answer File** to create a new answer file. The Answer File display pane shows the Components and Packages sections of the answer file.

9. Under Windows Longhorn SERVERENTERPRISE in the Windows Image pane, open the **components** folder.

10. Scroll down and highlight **x86_Microsoft-Windows-Shell-Setup_6.0.####.#####_neutral** (the numbers for ####.##### will vary depending on the version of Windows Server 2008 installed).

11. Right-click **x86_Microsoft-Windows-Shell-Setup_6.0.####.#####_neutral**, then click **Add Setting to Pass 7 oobeSystem**.

12. In the middle of the screen, in the Answer File section, highlight **x86_Microsoft-Windows-Shell-Setup_neutral**. This displays a number of base values in the Answer File Properties pane.

13. In the properties pane, highlight **StartPanelOff** and press **F1**. F1 launches the Unattended Windows Setup Reference window and displays details of the StartPanelOff setting.

14. Review the StartPanelOff help and close the Unattended Windows Setup Reference window.

15. Choose **True** from the drop-down menu next to StartPanelOff. This forces the classic Start menu view when an OS is built with this answer file.

16. Press **Ctrl + S** to save the answer file.

17. In the Save As window, type **2008AnswerFile** and click **Save**. This saves all settings changes to the XML answer file.

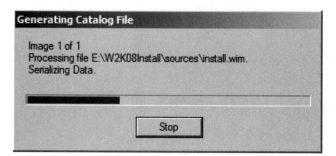

Figure 2-6   Generating an image catalog file in the WSIM

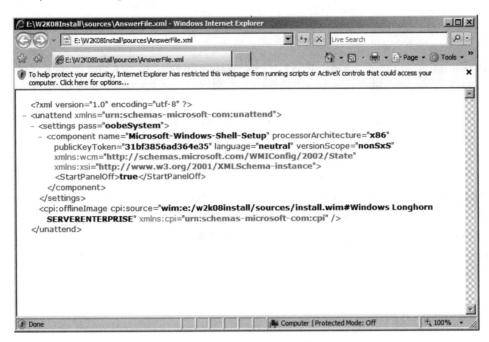

Figure 2-7   XML content of answer file in Internet Explorer

18. Click **Start, Run**, type **e:\W2K08Install\Sources\2008AnswerFile.xml**, and press **Enter** to open the answer file in Internet Explorer, as shown in Figure 2-7.

19. Close all open windows and log off your server.

Review Questions

1. How many component areas are available in a WSIM answer file?

   a. 2

   b. 7

   c. 14

   d. 51

2. This file format is used to store answer files.

   a. .wim

   b. .iso

   c. .csv

   d. .xml

3. Which of the following would be the most efficient method for getting help with a specific component setting?

   a. Search for the component name in your favorite search engine.

   b. Highlight the component setting and press F1.

   c. Double-click on the component setting.

   d. Highlight the component setting and click the Help icon on the taskbar.

4. Before you can load an image file into WSIM for creating an answer file, a _____ file must be created for the image file.

5. True or False? WSIM only needs DNS name resolution on the Internet in order to function properly.

NETWORKING WITH WINDOWS SERVER 2008

Labs included in this chapter

- Lab 3.1 Network Concepts Review
- Lab 3.2 Subnetting IPv4 Addresses
- Lab 3.3 Working with CIDR Addressing
- Lab 3.4 Researching Netsh Using Network Shell Reference Guide

Microsoft MCTS Exam #70-642 Objectives

Objective	Lab
Configuring IP Addressing and Services: Configure IPv4 and IPv6 Addressing	3.2, 3.3, 3.4

Lab 3.1 Network Concepts Review

The objective of this activity is to provide a refresher of networking terms used in Windows Server 2008 networking.

Materials Required

This lab requires the following:

- A pencil or pen, and paper

Estimated completion time: **15 minutes**

Activity Background

Before you can begin working with Windows networks, a good understanding of network components and concepts is necessary. It is important to understand the characteristics of and differences between the types of networks you'll be working with, such as local area networks and wide area networks. Equally important is an understanding of network components such as switches and routers. From there, you can move on to an understanding of IPv4 and IPv6, their differences, and how they are implemented.

1. Match the networking term to its definition.

1. Local area network:_____	a. The OSI model layer responsible for establishing paths for data transfer through the network. Routers operate at this layer.
2. Wide area network:_____	b. A network device that works at Layer 2 of the OSI model and forwards frames between ports based on MAC address.
3. Switch:_____	c. A device responsible for forwarding packets between subnets, or networks with differing IP addressing schemes.
4. Router:_____	d. The most basic of the hardware devices that interconnect multiple nodes.
5. Hub:_____	e. IPv6 transition technology that allows IPv6 hosts to communicate over IPv4 networks that use NAT.
6. Packet:_____	f. A transition technology where clients connected to an IPv4 network send IPv6 traffic over IPv4 by encapsulating the IPv6 traffic in an IPv4 packet.
7. Node:_____	g. A network connecting computers within very large areas, such as states, countries, and the world.
8. Network:_____	h. A network covering a small geographic area, such as a home, office, or building.
9. IPv6 over IPv4:_____	i. A unit of data routed between a sender and a receiver on the Internet or any other packet-switched network.
10. Teredo:_____	j. A computer or hardware device that participates in a network.

2. Describe the differences between IPv4 and IPv6 addresses, including their notation, base numbering scheme, and an example of each.

_____

_____

_____

_____

_____

Certification Objectives

Objectives for MCTS Exam #70-642: Windows Server 2008 Network Infrastructure, Configuration:

- Configuring IP Addressing and Services: Configure IPv4 and IPv6 Addressing

Review Questions

1. Which of the following is required for computers on different subnets to communicate?

   a. hub

   b. router

   c. repeater

   d. switch

2. Which layer of the OSI model is used by routers?

   a. Transport

   b. Network

   c. Presentation

   d. Physical

3. Which of the following is the simplified IPv6 address of 1065:1111:0000:001d:0000:0000:300c:422d?

   a. 1065:1111::001d::300c:422d

   b. 1065:1111::1d::300c:422d

   c. 1065:1111:0000:001d::300c:422d

   d. 1065:1111:0:1d::300c:422d

4. True or False? When shortening IPv6 addresses, you may use "::" more than once when replacing two or more groups of zeroes.

5. The typical small office (single building) network is considered a _____ area network.

Lab 3.2 Subnetting IPv4 Addresses

Objectives

The objective of this activity is to practice subnetting IPv4 addresses.

Materials Required

This lab requires the following:

- A pencil or pen, and paper

Estimated completion time: **15 minutes**

Activity Background

A solid foundation of networking knowledge requires a good understanding of IP addressing. IPv4 addresses, as you have learned, are based on an addressing scheme that uses unique 32-bit (4-byte) addresses. IPv4 addresses are displayed using dotted-decimal notation such as 192.168.100.254 or 10.1.1.5. These addresses are used by network devices for routing traffic between nodes, determining the senders of communication, and more. Originally, IP addresses were assigned using classes for the IP ranges, often called classful IP addressing. The commonly used ranges are Class A, Class B, and Class C. This led to a shortage of public IP addresses due to the rapid expansion of the Internet. Although not used as commonly as its replacement, CIDR, knowledge of the classful system of IP addressing is important for building a strong networking background.

Activity

1. Complete Table 3-1, describing the characteristics of the classful IP address ranges of Class A, Class B, and Class C.

2. Complete Table 3-2 by determining the network ID for each IP address along with the number of hosts per subnet.

Table 3-1

Classful address range	Range of addresses in class	Number of bits used by network ID	Number of bits used for hosts	Default subnet mask
Class A				
Class B				
Class C				

Table 3-2

IPv4 address	Subnet mask	Network ID of address	Number of hosts per subnet
101.26.34.10	255.0.0.0		
201.5.43.254	255.255.255.0		
165.33.222.18	255.255.0.0		

Certification Objectives

Objectives for MCTS Exam #70-642: Windows Server 2008 Network Infrastructure, Configuration:

- Configuring IP Addressing and Services: Configuring IPv4 and IPv6 Addressing

Review Questions

1. How many classes for special-use IPv4 addresses are defined by RFC 3330?

   a. 2

   b. 3

   c. 4

   d. 5

2. Which of the following IP addresses is a Class C address?

   a. 125.105.4.32

   b. 172.1.13.12

   c. 192.32.13.12

   d. 191.32.13.12

3. Which of the following is not a private IP address?

   a. 10. 15.14.13

   b. 172.15.14.13

   c. 172.30.29.28

   d. 192.168.10.9

4. True or False? Currently, classful addressing meets the IP needs of the Internet.

5. In binary numbering, the number one (1) represents _____ or _____.

Lab 3.3 Working with CIDR Addressing

The objective of this activity is to practice working with CIDR-based IP address ranges.

Materials Required

This lab requires the following:

- A pencil or pen, and paper

Estimated completion time: **15 minutes**

Activity Background

When it was determined that the use of the classful system was leading to a shortage of IP addresses, the **Classless Interdomain Routing**, or **CIDR**, system was put into place. CIDR deals with the limitations of classful addressing by allowing the allocation of IP addresses based on need, not general classification. CIDR uses variable-length subnet masks to provide individualized network addressing. CIDR addresses use an IP network address and the "/" character followed by the number of bits allocated to the network portion of the address.

An example would be 192.168.200.0 /28. With 28 bits allocated to the network ID (similar to a subnet mask of 255.255.255.240), you can split a typical Class C address into multiple smaller subnets. In this case, you have 16 available networks with 14 hosts per network.

Activity

1. Using the table below, determine the CIDR network mask and the CIDR-notated network ID for the given classful IP addresses.

Custom Subnet Masks Using CIDR

Network ID	Default subnet mask (Classful)	Number of subnets desired	CIDR network mask	CIDR notated network ID	Hosts per subnet
192.168.100.0	255.255.255.0	6			
205.1.1.0	255.0.0.0	4			
192.100.1.0	255.255.0.0	25			
220.20.1.0	255.255.0.0	2			

Certification Objectives

Objectives for MCTS Exam #70-642: Windows Server 2008 Network Infrastructure, Configuration:

- Configuring IP Addressing and Services: Configure IPv4 and IPv6 Addressing

Review Questions

1. CIDR stands for _____.

   a. Class full Interdomain Routing

   b. Class-based Interdomain Routing

   c. Classless Internet Routing

   d. Classless Interdomain Routing

2. Which of the following is not a subnet contained within the network ID of 192.80.70.0 /26?

   a. 192.80.70.0

   b. 192.80.70.32

   c. 192.80.70.64

   d. 192.80.70.192

3. How many useable IP addresses are available in the subnet of 192.80.70.96 /27?

   a. 14

   b. 30

   c. 62

   d. 96

4. Which of the following IP addresses are on the same subnet when using a /28 mask? (Choose all that apply.)

   a. 192.168.100.12

   b. 192.168.100.18

   c. 192.168.100.25

   d. 192.168.100.33

   e. 192.168.100.49

5. In order to divide 192.168.100.0 into 16 subnets, you use a _____ net mask.

Lab 3.4 Researching Netsh Using Network Shell Reference Guide

Objective

The objective of this activity is to review the Netsh command and become familiar with the Network Shell Reference Guide.

Materials Required

This lab requires the following:

- A USB drive or other removable media for storing files.
- The physical computer or virtual machine running Windows Server 2008, Enterprise (Full Edition) that was previously configured as LABSRVXX, or another name specified by your instructor. One network adapter will be connected to a private network and one adapter will be connected to an Internet-accessible network as follows:
  - Local Area Connection uses DHCP and connects to the Internet. If DHCP is not available, statically set the IP address configuration of this adapter.
  - Local Area Connection 2 connects to a private network or virtual network (if using virtualization).

Estimated completion time: **45 minutes**

Activity Background

While many administrators use the GUI to configure networking components in Windows Server 2008, the Network Shell, or Netsh, scripting utility is a powerful command-line utility. Netsh commands can be run from the netsh prompt, compiled in batch files or scripts, or issued as a single command at the command prompt. Administrators find Netsh invaluable when administering Windows Server 2008 computers running Server Core, which requires Netsh to configure network components and remote computers.

Activity

Microsoft provides a large number of technical resources for Server 2008, and the Netsh command is no exception. Using www.microsoft.com/downloads, search for **Windows Server 2008 Network Shell (Netsh) Technical Reference** and download the **Netsh.exe** to your local machine. Running this executable will extract the Compiled HTML Help File for Netsh, netsh.chm. Review the Netsh Overview, Enter a Netsh Context, Formatting Legend, and Netsh Commands for Interface (IPv4 and IPv6) sections to answer the following review questions. Keep a copy of netsh.chm for future reference on topics such as Windows Firewall and DHCP.

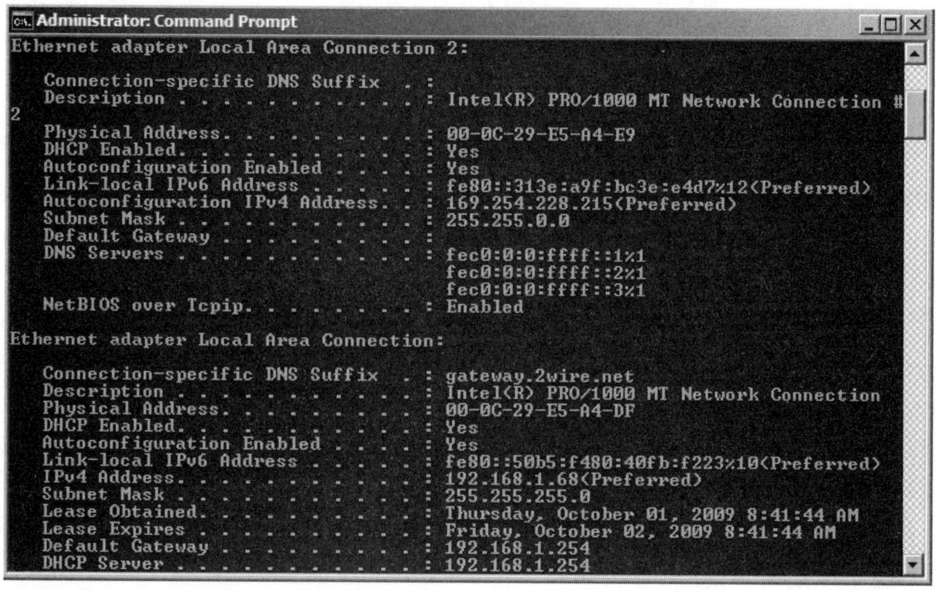

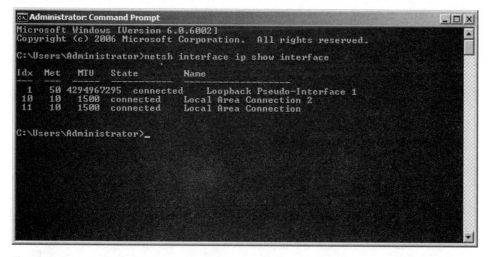

Figure 3-1 IP configuration of Windows Server 2008 computer with two network adapters

Upon completion of your research, complete the following steps on LABSRVXX using Netsh.

1. Log on to LABSRVXX.

2. Open the command prompt from the Start menu.

3. Enter **ipconfig /all**. You should see a screen similar to Figure 3-1. Note the 169.254.228.215 IP address on Local Area Connection 2. It falls in the APIPA range of addresses, which means the connection is set to use DHCP, but a server is not available.

4. Enter **netsh interface ip show interface**. The index number for each network connection displays as shown in Figure 3-2.

5. Enter **netsh interface set interface name="Local Area Connection" newname="Internet Connection"**.

6. Enter **netsh interface set interface name="Local Area Connection 2" newname="Netlab Network"**.

7. Enter **ipconfig /all**. Verify that the output now lists the names added in the above steps for each adapter.

8. Enter **netsh int ipv4 set addr "Netlab Network" static 192.168.1.201 255.255.255.0**. This sets the IP address on the private network adapter.

9. Enter **ipconfig /all**. Verify that the output now lists 192.168.1.201 as the IP address for the Netlab Network Ethernet Adapter.

Figure 3-2 Using Netsh to view the network interfaces on Windows Server 2008

10. Enter `ping 4.2.2.1`. Verify that you receive a successful reply back. If not, work with your instructor to resolve network connectivity issues.

11. Log off LABSRVXX.

Certification Objectives

Objectives for MCTS Exam #70-642: Windows Server 2008 Network Infrastructure, Configuration:

- Configuring IP Addressing and Services: Configure IPv4 and IPv6 Addressing

Review Questions

1. Which of the following will successfully run from the netsh interface IPv4> prompt?

   a. set address name=Local Area Connection source=static addr=192.168.100.101 mask=255.255.255.0 gateway=192.168.100.254 gwmetric=1

   b. set address name="Local Area Connection" source=dhcp addr=192.168.100.101 mask=255.255.255.0 gateway=192.168.100.254 gwmetric=1

   c. set address name="Local Area Connection" source=static addr=192.168.100.101 mask=255.255.255.0 gateway=192.168.100.254 gwmetric=1

   d. set address "Local Area Connection" source=dhcp addr=192.168.100.101 mask=255.255.255.0 gateway=192.168.100.254 gwmetric=1

2. Which of the following commands will not provide help information about netsh when run from the command prompt?

   a. netsh ?

   b. netsh /?

   c. netsh help

   d. netsh /help

3. Which of the following is not a proper netsh context command?

   a. firewall

   b. DHCPserver

   c. DHCPclient

   d. interface

4. True or False? Netsh can be run from a shell or the command prompt; it cannot be used for scripting multiple commands.

5. The _____ context is used for setting a static IPv4 address for a local network adapter.

INSTALLING AND
CONFIGURING DHCP

Labs included in this chapter

- Lab 4.1 Installing Active Directory
- Lab 4.2 Installing and Authorizing DHCP in an Active Directory Domain Services Domain
- Lab 4.3 Using Netsh to Configure DHCP
- Lab 4.4 Performing Backup and Restore with DHCP
- Lab 4.5 Implementing High-Availability DHCP

Microsoft MCTS Exam #70-642 Objectives

Objective	Lab
Configuring IP Addressing and Services: Configure Dynamic Host Configuration Protocol	4.2, 4.3, 4.4, 4.5

Lab 4.1 Installing Active Directory

Objectives

The object of this activity is to configure Active Directory Domain Services and configure the first domain controller in a domain.

Materials Required

This lab requires the following:

- The physical computer or virtual machine running Windows Server 2008, Enterprise (Full Edition) that was previously configured as LABSRVXX, or another name specified by your instructor.

Estimated completion time: **30 minutes**

Activity Background

Active Directory Domain Services (AD DS) provides centralized administration for Windows Server 2008 domains. Although DHCP can be installed into a workgroup environment, most scenarios will involve installing DHCP into an AD DS domain. In these environments, DHCP, DNS, and AD DS are tightly integrated.

Activity

1. Log on to LABSRVXX. In Server Manager, right-click **Roles** and then click **Add Roles**.

2. If the Before You Begin page opens, place a check mark in the **Skip this page by default** check box and click **Next**.

3. Click the box next to **Active Directory Domain Services** and then click **Next**.

4. Review the Introduction to Active Directory Domain Services and then click **Next**.

5. In the Confirm Installation Selections window, review the selections and then click **Install** to begin installing the AD DS role. To install a fully functional DC, you need to run the AD DS Installation Wizard, or dcpromo.exe, after the role is installed.

6. In the Installation Results window, click the blue **Close this wizard and launch the Active Directory Domain Services Installation Wizard (dcpromo.exe)** link as shown in Figure 4-1.

7. When the Active Directory Domain Services Installation Wizard starts, click **Next** to begin the installation. In the Operating System Compatibility dialog box, click **Next** to accept the defaults.

8. Click the **Create a new domain in a new forest** option button and then click **Next**.

9. In the Name the Forest Root Domain dialog box, enter **netlab.local** as the fully qualified domain name (FQDN) of the forest root domain and then click **Next**.

10. In the Set Forest Functional Level dialog box, choose **Windows Server 2008** in the Forest functional level text box and then click **Next**. In the Additional Domain Controller Options dialog box, click **Next** without adding controller options.

11. If a Static IP address assignment warning appears, choose **Yes, the computer will use a dynamically assigned IP address (not recommended)**. This dialog box appears if you are using virtualization software, running Windows Server 2008 on a computer with multiple network adapters that are not all statically assigned, or using Dynamic Host Configuration Protocol (DHCP) reservations for IP address assignments to your DCs.

12. If a delegation credentials message appears as shown in Figure 4-2, click **Yes**. This error appears as you are installing Active Directory into a domain without an existing DNS infrastructure, which is normal when installing the first Domain Controller.

13. Click **Next** to accept the default locations for the database, log files, and SYSVOL folder.

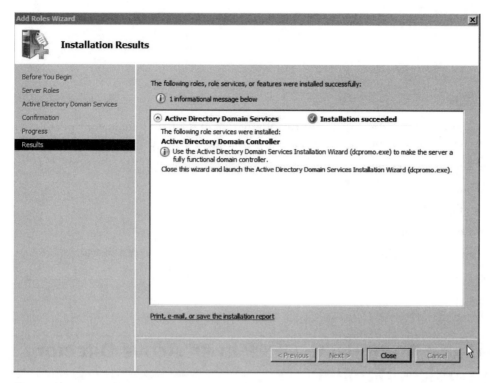

Figure 4-1   Active Directory Domain Services Installation Results window

Figure 4-2   Delegation credentials message box

14. Type **P@ssw0rd** as the Directory Services Restore Mode administrator password and then click **Next**. This password is crucial to restoring an AD database from backup files.

15. In the Summary dialog box, click **Next**. The installation wizard begins.

16. In the Completing Active Directory Domain Services Installation Wizard dialog box, click **Finish**. To reboot your computer to finish the installation, click **Restart Now** in the message box.

17. When the server reboots, wait 15 minutes before proceeding to the next activity. This allows AD DS to complete its post-installation routine.

Review Questions

1. Which of the following applications is used to complete the domain controller creation process?

   a. DCcreate.exe

   b. PromoDC.exe

   c. DCpromo.msi

   d. DCpromo.exe

2. Which of the following roles or features is required to run Active Directory?

   a. DHCP

   b. DNS

   c. WINS

   d. Windows PowerShell

3. Which of the following is not performed during the installation of the first domain controller on a network, assuming that Windows Server 2008 does not have any roles or features currently installed?

   a. Install Active Directory Domain Services Role

   b. Install and Configure DNS

   c. Install and Configure DHCP

   d. Run Domain Controller promotion process

4. True or False? Domain controllers should always use a static IP address instead of using DHCP.

5. The Active Directory Restore Mode password is required for restoring the _____ database.

Lab 4.2 Installing and Authorizing DHCP in an Active Directory Domain Services Domain

Objectives

The objective of this activity is to install the DHCP service and authorize the service for use in an AD DS domain environment.

Materials Required

This lab requires the following:

- The physical computer or virtual machine running Windows Server 2008, Enterprise (Full Edition) that was previously configured as LABSRVXX, or another name specified by your instructor.

Estimated completion time: **25 minutes**

Activity Background

DHCP is the industry-standard protocol used on networks for the dynamic allocation of IP addresses to network clients. Without DHCP, administrators would be required to manually set IP addresses for clients. DHCP can work in workgroup or domain environments. Unlike installing DHCP into a workgroup environment, installing DHCP in a domain requires the additional steps of authorizing the DHCP server.

Activity

1. Log on to LABSRVXX.

2. Open Server Manager, if necessary, right-click **Roles**, and then click **Add Roles**.

3. In the Add Roles Wizard, select **Dynamic Host Configuration Protocol (DHCP)**. If a Static IP address assignment warning appears, choose **Install DHCP Server anyway (not recommended)** and click **Next**. This warning appears because LABSRVXX is a multi-homed server with one network adapter set for DHCP.

In a real world scenario, you would not want to install DHCP on a server that does not have a static IP address.

4. On the Introduction to DHCP Server screen, click **Next**.

5. If the Select Network Connection Bindings screen appears, click **Next**.

6. In the Specify IPv4 DNS Server Settings dialog box, click **Next**. Because you are installing DHCP on a domain controller, the parent domain and preferred DNS server are already populated.

7. In the Specify IPv4 WINS Server Settings dialog box, click **Next**. This installs DHCP without requiring support for WINS.

8. In the Add or Edit DHCP Scopes dialog box, click **Add**.

9. Use the following information to complete the Add Scope window as shown in Figure 4-3. When completed, click **OK** and then click **Next**.

    Scope Name: Netlab Subnet 192.168.1.0 /Net - Wireless

    Starting IP Address: 192.168.1.1

    Ending IP Address: 192.168.1.126

    Subnet Mask: 255.255.255.128

    Default Gateway: 192.168.1.1

    Subnet Type: Wireless

10. In the Configure DHCPv6 Stateless Mode dialog box, choose **Disable DHCPv6 stateless mode for this server** and then click **Next**.

11. On the Authorize DHCP Server screen, click **Next** to use the current credentials for authorizing DHCP. Because the default Administrator account is a member of the Enterprise Admins global group, it will authorize the server in AD DS.

12. Review the settings in the Confirm Installation Settings dialog box and then click **Install** to begin the installation process.

13. When the installation is complete, click **Close** to exit the wizard.

Certification Objectives

Objectives for MCTS Exam #70-642: Windows Server 2008 Network Infrastructure, Configuration:

- Configuring IP Addressing and Services: Configure Dynamic Host Configuration Protocol

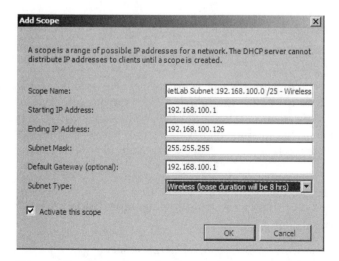

Figure 4-3 Add Scope window from DHCP Role installation wizard

Review Questions

1. Which group membership is required in order to authorize a DHCP server in an Active Directory domain?

   a. Schema Admin groups

   b. Administrators group

   c. Domain Admins group

   d. Enterprise Admins group

2. Which information is not requested during the Add Role Wizard process with DHCP?

   a. IPv4 DNS Settings

   b. IPv4 WINS Settings

   c. Install location of database

   d. DHCP Stateless mode preference

3. You are troubleshooting reasons why a DHCP server is not providing IPv4 addresses. In order to rule out possibilities, you log on to the server to verify if the server is authorized. How will you know the server is authorized?

   a. Verify that the Authorize Server checkbox is set on the server properties page.

   b. Verify that there is a green arrow next to the IPv4 server icon.

   c. Verify that the Authorize Server checkbox is set on the IPV4 properties page.

   d. Verify that the Status of DHCP is Authorized in the DHCP console.

4. True or False? Workgroup installations of DHCP require authorization before they can provide IP addresses to clients.

5. DHCP installations on a _____ network do not require authorization.

Lab 4.3 Using Netsh to Configure DHCP

Objectives

The objective of this activity is to configure a DHCP server from the command prompt using Netsh.exe.

Materials Required

This lab requires the following:

- The physical computer or virtual machine running Windows Server 2008, Enterprise (Full Edition) that was previously configured as LABSRVXX, or another name specified by your instructor.

Estimated completion time: **15 minutes**

Activity Background

DHCP uses scopes to manage the allocation of IP addresses. A scope is usually encompassed by a single subnet or part of a subnet. Along with the available IP addresses for the subnet, scopes provide information such as the default gateways and DNS servers to be used by clients.

Network Shell, or Netsh, is a built-in command line shell for managing various network configurations. In the case of DHCP, it can be used to create and configure a DHCP scope along with other DHCP settings.

Activity

Using the command prompt and Netsh, create a scope based on the following information for LABSRVXX:

Name of Scope: Netlab Wired Scope – 192.168.1.128 /25

Description: This is the scope for the wired network on 192.168.1.128 /25 subnet

Scope Subnet: 192.168.1.128 /25

IP Address Range: 192.168.1.129-254

Exclusionary Range: 192.168.1.200-254

DNS Servers: 192.168.1.201, 192.168.1.202

Gateway Routers: 192.168.1.254, 192.168.1.253

1. Log on to LABSRVXX.

2. Open the command prompt and enter **netsh dhcp server show all** to display the current status of the DHCP server including information about the current scope.

3. Enter **netsh dhcp server 192.168.1.201 add scope 192.168.1.128 255.255.255.128 "NetLab Wired Scope - 192.168.1.128/25"**. This creates a new scope on your DHCP server.

4. Enter **netsh dhcp server 192.168.1.201 scope 192.168.1.128 add iprange 192.168.1.129 192.168.1.254**. This adds a range of IP addresses to the scope you just created.

5. Enter **netsh dhcp server 192.168.1.201 scope 192.168.1.128 add excluderange 192.168.1.200 192.168.1.254**. This creates an exclusionary range in your scope.

6. Enter **netsh dhcp server 192.168.1.201 scope 192.168.1.128 set optionvalue 003 IPADDRESS 192.168.1.254 192.168.1.253**. This adds a scope option that sets the default gateway routers.

7. Enter **netsh dhcp server 192.168.1.201 scope 192.168.1.128 set optionvalue 006 IPADDRESS 192.168.1.201 192.168.1.202**. This adds a scope option that sets the DNS servers to be used by clients.

8. Enter **netsh dhcp server 192.168.1.201 scope 192.168.1.128 set state 1**. This activates the DHCP scope.

9. Enter **netsh dhcp server show scope > DHCPScopes.txt. This sends the output of the Netsh server to a text file for easier viewing**.

Certification Objectives

Objectives for MCTS Exam #70-642: Windows Server 2008 Network Infrastructure, Configuration:

- Configuring IP Addressing and Services: Configure Dynamic Host Configuration Protocol

Review Questions

1. Which of the following commands will create a new DHCP scope for 10.1.1.0 /27 on DHCP Server 10.1.1.101?

   a. netsh dhcp server 10.1.1.101 add scope 10.1.1.0 255.255.255.224 "Wired Scope – 10.1.1.0 /27".

   b. netsh dhcp server 10.1.1.101 add scope 10.1.1.0 255.255.255.240 "Wired Scope – 10.1.1.0 /27".

   c. netsh dhcp 10.1.1.101 add scope 10.1.1.0 255.255.255.224 "Wired Scope – 10.1.1.0 /27".

   d. netsh dhcp 10.1.1.101 add scope 10.1.1.0 255.255.255.240 "Wired Scope – 10.1.1.0 /27".

   e. netsh dhcp server 10.1.1.101 add scope 10.1.101.0 255.255.255.224 "Wired Scope – 10.1.1.0 /27".

2. Which of the following are not displayed by **netsh dhcp server show all**?

   a. Database backup path

   b. Subnets of scopes

   c. Percent of IP addresses free

   d. IP addresses in use

3. What directory is the default location for the DHCP installation?

   a. c:\Windows\System\DHCP

   b. c:\Windows\System32\DHCP

   c. c:\Windows\System32\DHCPServer

   d. c:\Windows\System\DHCPServet

4. Which of the following are displayed by netsh dhcp server scope?

   a. IP Addresses in use

   b. Number of Scopes

   c. State of Scope

   d. Percent of IP addresses free

   e. a and d

   f. b and c

   g. All of the above

5. The **netsh dhcp server** _____ command will display all of the commands available for use with **netsh dhcp server**.

Lab 4.4 Performing Backup and Restore with DHCP

Objectives

The objective of this activity is to perform backup and restore tasks on a DHCP Server.

Materials Required

This lab requires the following:

- The physical computer or virtual machine running Windows Server 2008, Enterprise (Full Edition) that was previously configured as LABSRVXX, or another name specified by your instructor.

Estimated completion time: **15 minutes**

Activity Background

Backup and restore for DHCP is a fairly simple process. With a few simple commands, you can quickly back up your DHCP database to a location of your choice. Restores are performed much the same way. Both utilize **netsh dhcp server** commands to perform their duties.

1. Log on to LABSRVXX.

2. Open a command prompt window.

3. Enter **netsh dhcp server dump > DHCPDump.txt**. This dumps the DHCP configuration of the current server to a text file.

4. Enter **DHCPDump.txt** and review the text file. This opens the text file of the DHCP configuration in Notepad.

5. Enter **netsh dhcp server backup c:\Chapter4\DHCPBackup**. This backs up the DHCP database.

6. Open Windows Explorer and Browse to **c:\Chapter4\DHCPBackup\new**. Verify that the folder contains files similar to those shown in Figure 4-4.

7. Open the DHCP console and delete all scopes under LABSRVXX. Close the DHCP Console.

8. In the command prompt window, type **Netsh dhcp server restore c:\Chapter4\DHCPBackup**. This restores the DHCP database from the previous backup you created.

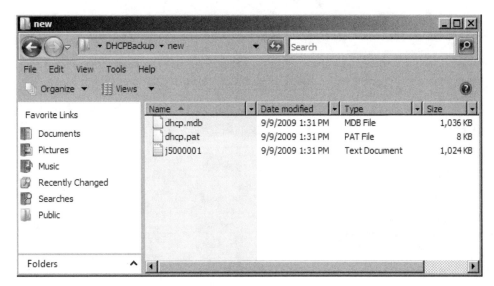

Figure 4-4   DHCP database files created by manual backup task

9. Enter **Net stop dhcpserver and Net start dhcpserver** to restart the DHCP Server service. This is necessary whenever you restore the DHCP database.

10. Open the DHCP Console and verify that all the scopes deleted in Step 7 above have returned.

Certification Objectives

Objectives for MCTS Exam #70-642: Windows Server 2008 Network Infrastructure, Configuration:

- Configuring IP Addressing and Services: Configure Dynamic Host Configuration Protocol

Review Questions

1. What is the default location for automatic DHCP backups?

    a. c:\Windows\System\DHCP\backup

    b. c:\Windows\System32\DHCPServer\backup

    c. c:\Windows\System32\DHCP\backup

    d. c:\Windows\System\DHCPServer\backup

2. How often are automatic backups performed on a DHCP server?

    a. Every 30 minutes

    b. Every 45 minutes

    c. Every 60 minutes

    d. Every 90 minutes

3. What is the default location for manual DHCP backups?

    a. c:\Windows\System32\DHCPServer\backup

    b. c:\Windows\System32\DHCP\backup

    c. c:\Windows\System\DHCP\backup

    d. c:\Windows\System\DHCPServer\backup

4. True or False? In the case of a total server failure, you would not be able to restore a DHCP server to its previous state unless you had a manual backup.

5. For full system recovery, backups should be stored on the _____ so they are available if a system fails and data is not available on the hard drives.

Lab 4.5 Implementing High-Availability DHCP

Objectives

The objective of this activity is to design a high-availability implementation plan for DHCP.

Materials Required

This lab requires the following:

- A pencil or pen, and paper
- A word processing application

Estimated completion time: **30 minutes**

Activity Background

Without IP addresses, clients will not be able to access resources on the network. Like many roles in Windows Server 2008, DHCP can be set up for high-availability and fault tolerance on your network. There are a number of options for setting this up using tools contained within Windows Server 2008.

Activity

You have been hired by Badger Components as a consultant. The company is currently running Windows Server 2008 and has a single DHCP server that contains 20 scopes. As part of a company audit, DHCP was listed as a service requiring high availability within the environment. You have been asked to develop an implementation plan for adding high availability to the company's DHCP service. Describe any additional hardware required, and the steps you would take to implement your solution.

Certification Objectives

Objectives for MCTS Exam #70-642: Windows Server 2008 Network Infrastructure, Configuration:

- Configuring IP Addressing and Services: Configure Dynamic Host Configuration Protocol

Review Questions

1. Which of following are built-in roles and features of Windows Server 2008 that can assist with making DHCP highly available?

    a. Hyper-V

    b. Failover clustering

    c. Network load balancing

    d. All of the above

2. Which of the following steps would not be performed when setting up two DHCP servers for fault tolerance?

    a. Set the DHCP relay agent/router to use both servers

    b. Split the scopes between each server so no IP ranges overlap

    c. Set up DHCP replication so the servers maintain up-to-date records and configurations

    d. Verify that your current IP scheme will support failover to one DHCP server

3. You have two servers, DHCP1 and DHCP2, that will be responsible for maintaining DHCP on your network. Because of hardware specs, DHCP1 will be the primary server, and DHCP2 will be a secondary, providing fault tolerance in case of a failure on DHCP1. Given the following subnets, what is the proper split of IP addresses when using the 80/20 rule?

   192.168.1.0 /24

   192.168.2.0 /24

   a. DHCP1: 192.168.1.0-203,192.168.2.0-203; DHCP2: 192.168.1.204-254, 192.168.204-254

   b. DHCP1: 192.168.1.1-203,192.168.2.1-203; DHCP2: 192.168.1.204-254, 192.168.204-254

   c. DHCP1: 192.168.1.1-203,192.168.2.1-203; DHCP2: 192.168.1.204-255, 192.168.204-255

   d. DHCP1: 192.168.1.203-254,192.168.2.203-254; DHCP2: 192.168.1.1-203, 192.168.1-203

4. True or False? Implementing a high availability solution will guarantee you have no downtime.

5. _____ is an installable feature of Windows Server 2008. It allows you to set up an additional server to act as a stand-in if your primary server fails.

INTRODUCTION TO DNS IN WINDOWS SERVER 2008

Labs included in this chapter

- Lab 5.1 Building and Configuring a Server Running Windows Server Core
- Lab 5.2 Building a Primary DNS Server on LABSCXX
- Lab 5.3 Managing Server Core DNS Remotely Using DNS Console
- Lab 5.4 Configuring DNS with Dnscmd
- Lab 5.5 Creating DNS Records

Microsoft MCTS Exam #70-642 Objectives

Objective	Lab
Configure Name Resolution: Configure a Domain Name System (DNS) server	5.2
Configure Name Resolution: Configure DNS zones	5.2, 5.3, 5.4
Configure Name Resolution: Configure DNS records	5.4, 5.5
Configure Name Resolution: Configure DNS replication	5.4

Lab 5.1 Building and Configuring a Server Running Windows Server Core

Objectives

The objective of this activity is to build and configure a server running Windows Server Core.

Materials Required

This lab requires the following:

- Physical computer or virtual machine that meets the requirements for running Windows Server 2008 including a single network adapter. This lab is designed to work in physical or virtual machine lab environments.
- Network connectivity to partner machine, LABSRVXX

Estimated completion time: **45 minutes**

Activity Background

As you know, Windows Server 2008 includes a new type of Windows Server installation called Server Core. This is a scaled-down version of Windows Server 2008 that provides a reduced attack surface and limited role and feature hosting abilities. Server Core provides no GUI with the exception of tools like Notepad, Regedit, and the Time and Date console. You perform all configuration and administration tasks locally from the command prompt or remotely using tools such as WinRM and Microsoft Management Consoles. Because Server Core has a limited role and feature set, along with fewer installed services, it is a more secure server from the outset.

Activity

1. Place your Windows Server 2008 DVD in the DVD drive of your computer and then restart or power on your computer.

2. If prompted by the startup screen, press any key to boot from the DVD. You are prompted only if the computer has an existing operating system. The first portion of the installation program starts.

3. At the Install Windows initial screen, confirm your time and currency format and that the keyboard layout is correct and then click **Next**.

4. When the next window appears, click **Install now**.

5. If the next window requests a product key, enter your key in the product key text box if you have one or leave this text box blank for now. You can install Server 2008 without a product key. If you are not prompted for a product key, skip to Step 7.

 Depending on the type of installation media and license model you are using, you might not be prompted for a product key.

6. Click to remove the check mark from the **Automatically activate Windows when I'm online** box and then click **Next**. If you did not enter a product key, a message box opens asking whether you want to enter a key. Click **No** to continue installing without a product key.

7. When the next window appears, select the version of Server 2008 you are installing. For this activity, choose **Windows Server 2008 Enterprise (Server Core Installation)**, check the **I have selected the edition of Windows that I purchased** check box, and then click **Next**.

8. When the next window appears, read the Microsoft Software License Terms and then select the **I accept the license terms** check box. Click **Next**.

9. When the next window appears, click **Custom** to perform a custom installation, which is the appropriate option for performing a new installation. Notice that the choice to upgrade is not available.

10. If necessary, when the next window appears, delete any existing partitions by completing the following steps:

   a. Click the partition you want to delete.

   b. Click the **Drive options (advanced)** link to display your partitioning options.

   c. Click **Delete**.

   d. Click **OK** to confirm you want to delete the partition and lose all of its data.

11. Click **Disk 0 Unallocated Space** and then click **Drive options (advanced)** to perform disk partitioning operations. Click **New**. Enter **21024** in the Size text box and ensure that you will have at least 10 GB of unallocated disk space remaining on the disk. Click **Apply**.

12. Select **Disk 0 Partition 1** and then click **Format**. Confirm that you understand all data will be lost when you format the partition by clicking **OK**.

13. Click **Next**. Windows begins performing tasks that do not require input, including rebooting the computer. This portion of the installation takes approximately 5 to 10 minutes.

14. When Windows completes its tasks and reboots, press **Ctrl+Alt+Del** to pass the security key sequence to your server. Click the single user called **Other User**.

15. When asked to enter a user account name and password. Enter **Administrator** as the account name and leave the password blank. You change the password in the next step. Click the **arrow** button.

16. A warning reminds you that you need to change your password before logging on for the first time. Click **OK**. Use **P@ssw0rd** as your new password. Enter the password twice to ensure it is correct. Confirm that your password has been changed by clicking the **arrow** button and then clicking **OK**.

17. When the desktop is prepared, the Server Core command prompt appears.

18. Type the following command and then press **Enter** to change the computer name to LABSCXX, as shown in Figure 5-1, and enter **Y** when prompted:

   Netdom renamecomputer %computername% /newname:LABSCxx

19. The system now requires a reboot so that the name change takes effect. Type the following command and then press **Enter** to reboot:

   shutdown /r /f /t 0

20. After the system reboots, press **Ctrl+Alt+Del**.

21. When the log on screen appears, log on as Administrator.

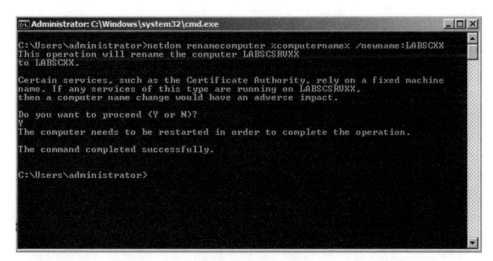

Figure 5-1   Using netdom to change the computer name in Windows Server 2008

5

 One interesting observation about Server Core systems is that the log on process can be much longer than Full versions of Windows Server 2008. This is counterintuitive because there is no GUI to build. Here's a tip for speeding up log on time with Server Core: After you have entered your credentials and are logging on, press **Ctrl+Alt+Del** and click **Cancel** when the Task Manager appears. By performing this sequence of steps, you can bypass waiting for the desktop to resolve and go right to the command prompt.

22. At the command prompt, type **hostname** and verify that the name has changed to LABSCXX.

23. Type **log off** and press **Enter** to exit LABSCXX.

Review Questions

1. Which type of DNS server is used to offload DNS query traffic for a zone? (Choose all that apply.)

   a. cache only

   b. primary

   c. secondary

   d. WINS

2. Which of the following top level domains is not usable on the Internet?

   a. .edu

   b. .net

   c. .priv

   d. .biz

3. True or False? Forwarders need to be created before a DNS server can act as a cache only DNS server.

4. Which of the following characters are not valid when creating a public DNS domain name? (Choose all that apply.)

   a. $

   b. -

   c. A

   d. b

   e. _

5. Prior to the proliferation of DNS servers, the _____ file was used to provide hostname to IP address resolution on client computers.

Lab 5.2 Building a Primary DNS Server on LABSCXX

Objectives

The objective of this activity is to install the DNS server role on Server Core and configure a standard primary DNS zone.

Materials Required

This lab requires the following:

- The LABSCXX computer configured in the previous activity.

Estimated completion time:	25 minutes

Activity Background

While most administration duties are performed through the GUI, Windows Server 2008 has many options for using the command line for administration, especially when working with Server Core. Besides using Netsh to

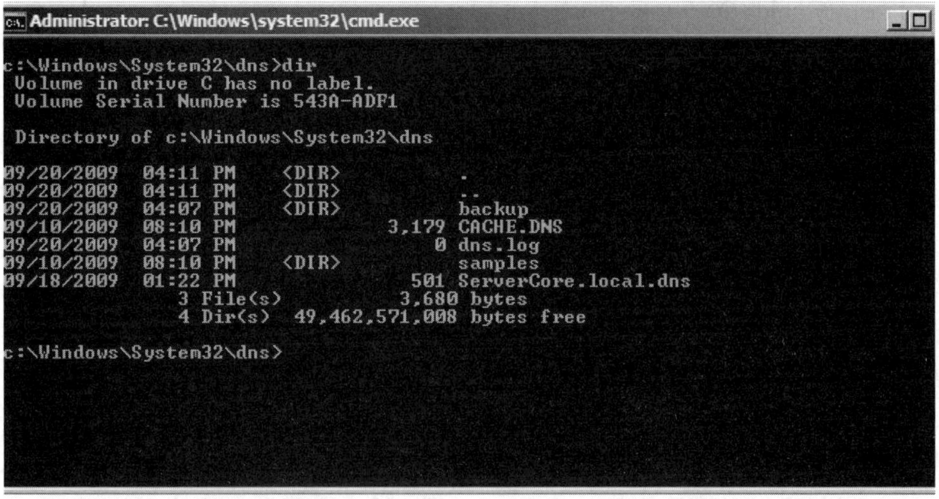

Figure 5-2   Contents of %systemroot%\system32\dns

configure networking settings, Ocsetup is used to install the DNS server role on Server Core installations. Once DNS is installed, Dnscmd is available to configure and manage a DNS server from the command line.

Activity

1. Log on to LABSCXX.

2. Enter **netsh interface set interface name="Local Area Connection" newname="Netlab Network"**. This network adapter will connect with LABSRVXX. Enter **netsh interface ipv4 set address "Netlab Network" static 192.168.1.202 255.255.255.0**. This sets the static IP address on Server Core.

3. Enter **netsh interface ipv4 add dnsserver "Netlab Network" 192.168.1.201 index=1**. This sets the DNS server for LABSCXX to LABSRVXX.

4. Enter **ocsetup DNS-Server-Core-Role** to install the DNS role on the Server Core machine.

5. Enter **net start** and scroll up until you see DNS Server listed. This command displays all of the started services and verifies that the DNS service is running.

6. Enter **dnscmd /info**. This allows you to view the DNS server information.

7. Enter **cd c:\Windows\System32\dns**, then Enter **dir** to view the contents of the DNS directory. This contains files and directories including dns.log, cache.dns, a backup directory, and any zone files for created zones.

8. Enter **DNScmd /zoneadd ServerCore.local /primary /file ServerCore.local.dns**. This adds a standard primary DNS zone for servercore.local on LABSCXX.

9. Enter **dir** to view the contents of the DNS directory. You should see a new file named ServerCore.local.dns, as shown in Figure 5-2.

10. Type **notepad servercore.local.dns** to view the DNS database file and the records stored within it. Close Notepad when you are done reviewing the database file.

11. Enter **log off** to exit LABSCXX.

Certification Objectives

Objectives for MCTS Exam #70-642: Windows Server 2008 Network Infrastructure, Configuration:

- Configure Name Resolution: Configure a Domain Name System (DNS) server
- Configure Name Resolution: Configure DNS zones

Review Questions

1. What utility is used to install DNS and other Roles/Features on Windows Server 2008 running Server Core?

   a. Oclist

   b. Servermanagercmd

   c. Ocsetup

   d. Server manager

2. By default, what directory holds DNS zone files?

    a. %systemroot%\system\dns

    b. c:\Program Data\DNS\zonefiles

    c. %systemroot%\system32\dns

    d. c:\windows\resources\dns

3. What utility is used to manage and configure DNS from the command line?

    a. Netsh

    b. Dnsconfig

    c. Servermanagercmd

    d. Dnscmd

4. Which of the following commands will add 192.168.100.101 as the alternate DNS server on a network adapter?

    a. netsh interface ipv4 add dnsserver "local area connection" 192.168.100.101 index=1

    b. netsh interface ipv4 add dnsserver "local area connection" 192.168.100.101 alternate

    c. netsh interface ipv4 add dnsserver "local area connection" 192.168.100.101 index=2

    d. netsh interface ipv4 add dnsserver "local area connection" 192.168.100.101

5. One of the risks of standard DNS zones is that they are file-based. In order to secure your standard DNS zone files, you need to modify the permissions to prevent non-authorized access. Which of the following files would you need to modify in order to secure the zone file for Badgerwidgets.local?

    a. C:\Windows\System\DNS\badgerwidgets.local.dns

    b. C:\Windows\System\DNS\badgerwidgets.local.zone

    c. C:\Windows\System32\DNS\badgerwidgets.local.dns

    d. C:\Windows\System32\DNS\cache.dns

Lab 5.3 Managing Server Core DNS Remotely Using DNS Console

Objectives

The objective of this activity is to remotely manage the DNS server role in Windows Server 2008.

Materials Required

This lab requires the following:

- The LABSRVXX computer configured in previous activities.
- The LABSCXX computer configured in previous activities.

Estimated completion time: **15 minutes**

Activity Background

Improved remote management capabilities is a major enhancement in Windows Server 2008 for network administrators. The Microsoft Management Console is one of the main tools administrators use to manage remote computers. Many of the consoles, including DNS, allow you to connect to a remote server and perform tasks on the remote server through the console.

In order to utilize remote management, administrators need to modify the Windows Firewall with Advanced Security to allow remote administration. By default, remote administration is blocked. This can be performed through the GUI or from the command line using the Netsh command with the advfirewall context.

Activity

1. Log on to LABSCXX.

2. Enter **netsh advfirewall firewall set rule group="remote administration" new enable=yes**. This will open the firewall to allow most remote management tools to access your server.

3. Log on to LABSRVXX.

4. Click **Start**, point to **Administrative Tools**, and click **DNS** to open DNS Manager. Click the **DNS** node, click **Action** on the menu bar, and then click **Connect to DNS Server**.

5. In the Connect to DNS Server message box, click **The following computer** option button, enter **192.168.1.202**, and then click **OK**. It might take a few minutes for the DNS server to resolve in the console.

6. Expand the **192.168.1.202** node until you reach the **Forward Lookup Zone** node. As you expand the nodes, you may have additional wait periods as the console is pulling the information from the remote system.

7. Click the **Show/Hide Action Pane** button on the menu bar. In the Actions pane, click **More Actions** and then click **New Zone** to start the New Zone Wizard. Click **Next**.

8. In the Zone Type dialog box, accept the default selection of a Primary Zone by clicking **Next**. Note that the Active Directory–integrated option is not available as the wizard will detect whether this action is being performed on a domain controller.

9. In the Zone Name dialog box, enter **RemoteZone.local** and then click **Next**.

10. In the Zone File dialog box, accept the default zone file name by clicking **Next**. Notice you can add existing files in this dialog box.

11. In the Dynamic Update dialog box, choose **Allow both nonsecure and secure dynamic updates** and then click **Next**.

12. Click **Finish** in the final dialog box to create the new zone for **RemoteZone.local**.

13. In the DNS console, click the **RemoteZone.local** folder within the Forward Lookup Zones to view the records in the zone.

14. In the DNS console, expand the **LABSRVXX** node, **Forward Lookup Zones**, and the **netlab.local** node and delete any Host(A) records for LABSRVXX that are not using the IP address 192.168.1.201. You should have only one if your server is currently connected to the Internet. (To delete a host record, right-click it and click **Delete**.)

15. Switch to LABSCXX.

16. Enter **dnscmd /enumzones**. This will enumerate the zones on LABSCXX. Note that ServerCore.local and RemoteZone.local are both listed.

17. Log off LABSCXX and LABSRVXX.

Certification Objectives

Objectives for MCTS Exam #70-642: Windows Server 2008 Network Infrastructure, Configuration:

- Configure Name Resolution: Configure DNS Zones
- Configure Name Resolution: Configure DNS Records

Review Questions

1. Which of the following are required to remotely configure a network DNS server?

   a. Installation of the Remote Server Administration Tools on the remote server

   b. Configuration of Windows Remote Management (WinRM) on both servers

   c. Modification of the Windows Firewall with Advanced Security on the remote server

   d. Membership in the same workgroup or domain

2. Which of the following zones provides host name-to-IP address resolution?

   a. Forward lookup zones

   b. Reverse lookup zones

   c. Stub zones

   d. Conditional forwarders

3. In order to resolve queries for IP address-to-host name resolution, the following needs to be created:

   a. Forward lookup zone

   b. Reverse lookup zone

   c. Stub zone

   d. Conditional forwarder

4. Using dnscmd _____ will list all of the dns zones available on a server.

5. True or False? A Windows Server 2008 DNS server will not perform any query operations unless at least one DNS zone is configured.

Lab 5.4 Configuring DNS with Dnscmd

Objectives

The objective of this activity is to configure a DNS server from the command prompt with dnscmd.exe.

Materials Required

This lab requires the following:

- The LABSCXX computer configured in previous activities.

Estimated completion time:	**30 minutes**

Activity Background

For DNS servers, Windows Server 2008 offers the command-line utility, Dnscmd. Dnscmd allows administrators to manage local or remote Windows Server 2008 computers from the command prompt. This is an excellent option for times when you need to perform a quick modification to DNS that is quicker from the command prompt, or when you are working with Server Core. Another excellent use of Dnscmd is for the bulk creation of DNS records.

Activity

1. Log on to LABSCXX.

2. Enter **dnscmd /zoneadd badgerwidgets.local /primary /file badgerwidgets.local. dns**. By not including a DNS server name prior to the /zoneadd command, dnscmd uses the local DNS server by default.

3. Enter **dnscmd /zoneprint badgerwidgets.local**. This lists the zone information for Badgerwidgets. local in the command prompt window as shown in Figure 5-3.

4. Enter **dnscmd /zoneresetsecondaries badgerwidgets.local /nonsecure**. This instructs the DNS server to allow zone transfers to anyone who asks.

5. Enter **dnscmd LABSRVXX.netlab.local /zoneadd badgerwidgets.local /secondary 192.168.1.202**. This command remotely creates a secondary DNS zone and instructs the zone to contact the primary server by its IP address.

6. Enter **dnscmd LABSRVXX.netlab.local /enumzones**. This enumerates the zones that are available on the remote server, LABSRVXX.

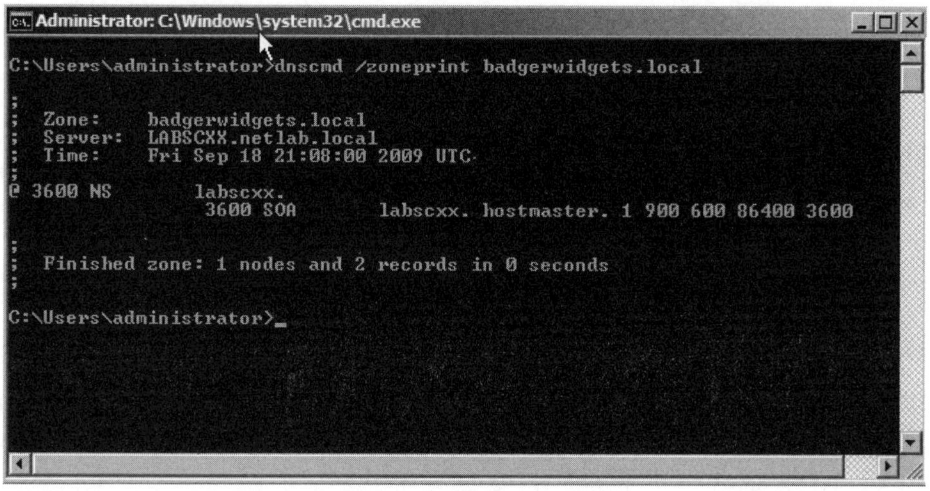

Figure 5-3 Viewing zone information from the command line

7. Enter **dnscmd LABSRVXX.netlab.local /recordadd netlab.local RemoteWks A 192.168.1.101**. This creates an A record on the remote server.

8. Enter **dnscmd /recordadd badgerwidgets.local comp1 A 192.168.100.101** to create an A record locally.

9. Enter **dnscmd LABSRVXX.netlab.local /zoneprint badgerwidgets.local**. Note that the recently created A record is not included because the information has not replicated yet.

10. Enter **dnscmd LABSRVXX.netlab.local /zonerefresh badgerwidgets.local** to manually force zone replication on the remote server.

11. Enter **dnscmd LABSRVXX.netlab.local /zoneprint badgerwidgets.local**. Now the record for comp1 appears as shown in Figure 5-4 because replication of the zone changes was forced.

12. Enter **dnscmd LABSRVXX.netlab.local /zoneprint netlab.local**. This might take a few minutes as it is running remotely and it is listing an Active Directory-integrated DNS zone so there are a lot of records to view.

13. Enter **dnscmd /recordadd badgerwidgets.local @ SOA DNS1.badgerwidgets.local BuckinghamB.badgerwidgets.local 1848 1200 900 86400 7200**. This modifies the Start of Authority record for badgerwidgets.local.

14. Enter **dnscmd /zoneprint badgerwidgets.local**. Note that the SOA record information has changed.

15. Enter **dnscmd /zonedelete remotezone.local /f** to delete the zone, remotezone.local, without asking for confirmation.

Figure 5-4 Viewing zone information from a remote DNS server

16. Enter **dnscmd /enumzones** to verify the remotezone.local has been removed from the DNS server.

17. Log off LABSCXX.

Certification Objectives

Objectives for MCTS Exam #70-642: Windows Server 2008 Network Infrastructure, Configuration:

- Configure Name Resolution: Configure DNS Records
- Configure Name Resolution: Configure DNS Replication

Review Questions

1. Which of the following commands will delete the dnszone, remotezone.local, on the DNS server, NS1.remotezone.local?

   a. dnscmd /zonedelete remotezone.local /Server NS1.remotezone.local

   b. dnscmd /deletezone remotezone.local

   c. dnscmd /zonedelete remotezone.local NS1.remotezone.local

   d. dnscmd NS1.remotezone.local /zonedelete remotezone.local

Based on the information in Figure 5-5, answer the following questions.

2. What command was used to produce this information on the server, Server1.netlab.local?

   a. Dnscmd /zoneprint *

   b. Dnscmd /info

   c. Dnscmd /zonelist

   d. Dnscmd /enumzones

3. How many zones exist on the DNS server?

   a. 2

   b. 3

   c. 4

   d. 5

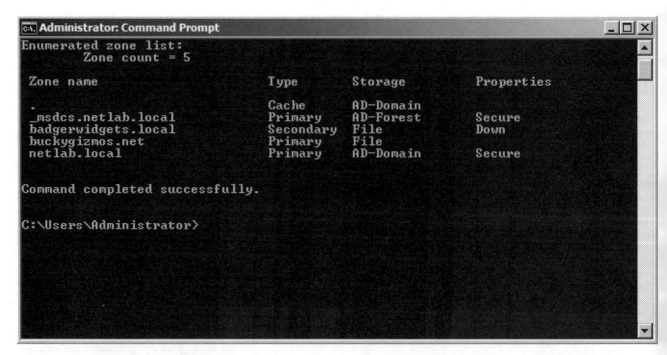

Figure 5-5   Command-line information

4. How many primary Active Directory-integrated zones exist on the DNS server?

   a. 2

   b. 3

   c. 4

   d. 5

5. True or False? Using the /f switch forces confirmation of all Dnscmd commands.

Lab 5.5 Creating DNS Records

Objectives

- The objective of this activity is to configure DNS records on a DNS server.

Materials Required

This lab requires the following:

- Physical computer or virtual machine running Windows Server 2008 with Internet access. This lab is designed to work in physical or virtual machine lab environments.

> Estimated completion time: **30 minutes**

Activity Background

In order for DNS to function, zones require records that resolve information for clients. Most often, DNS queries resolve the IP address for a specific host, using what is known as an A record. Besides host records, other common records include MX records for identifying mail servers and NS records for identifying name server records. These records can be created through the GUI using the DNS console or from the command line using Dnscmd. Both tools allow administration of records on remote DNS servers.

Activity:

1. Log on to LABSRVXX and start Server Manager, if necessary.

2. In the left pane of Server Manager on the LABSRVXX computer, expand **Roles** and then expand the **DNS Server** role until the netlab.local DNS zone folder is displayed. Click **netlab.local**.

3. Click **More Actions** in the Actions pane and then click **New Host (A or AAAA)**. The New Host window opens.

4. Enter **MSG001** as the host name and **192.168.1.50** as the IP address. Click **Add Host**, click **OK**, and then click Done.

5. Click **More Actions** in the Actions pane and then click **New Alias (CNAME)**. The New Resource Record window opens.

6. Enter **mail** as the alias name. This allows your internal clients to connect with the mail server by using a user-friendly name, mail.netlab.local.

 netlab.local is not a valid public domain name. The .local domain name is often used to differentiate internal domains from external domains.

7. Enter **MSG001** as the FQDN. This matches the alias with the appropriate A record. You can also browse to find the appropriate A record that matches the alias. Click **OK**.

8. Click **More Actions** in the Actions pane and then click **New Mail Exchanger (MX)**. The New Resource Record window opens.

9. In the "Fully qualified domain name (FQDN) of mail server" text box, enter **mail.netlab.local** for the FQDN of the mail server and then click **OK** to save the record. This is the name SMTP servers use when sending mail to netlab.local.

10. Log on to LABSCXX.

11. Enter **dnscmd /recordadd badgerwidgets.local test NS NS01.badgerwidgets.local** to create an additional Name Server (NS) record for badgerwidgets.local.

12. Enter **dnscmd /recordadd badgerwidgets.local mypc A 192.168.1.145** to create a hostname (A) record.

13. Enter **dnscmd /recordadd badgerwidgets.local @ MX 10 mail.badgerwidgets.local** to create a Mail Exchanger (MX) record for badgerwidgets.local.

14. Enter **dnscmd /zoneprint badgerwidgets.local**.

15. Enter **dnscmd /recorddelete badgerwidgets.local @ NS NS01.badgerwidgets.local /f**. This deletes the NS record you created above. Note that including "/f" at the end of the command suppresses deletion confirmation prompts.

16. Enter **dnscmd /zoneprint badgerwidgets.local**.

17. Enter **dnscmd /zonedelete badgerwidgets.local /f**.

18. Enter **dnscmd /enumzones**. Note the only remaining DNS zones are ".µ" and ServerCore.local.

19. Log off LABSCXX.

Certification Objectives

Objectives for MCTS Exam #70-642: Windows Server 2008 Network Infrastructure, Configuration:

- Configure Name Resolution: Configure DNS Records

Review Questions

1. You have just installed a new application server named NewAppServer1 to replace OldAppServer1. It is used by a desktop application, NewApp. NewApp needs to be configured to use the new server's hostname. After the initial application configuration, clients are unable to access NewApp1 by name. However, they can access the application by IP address. What do you do to resolve this issue?

   a. Create an entry in the HOSTS file on NewAppServer1

   b. Create a PTR record on your DNS servers for NewAppServer1

   c. Create an A record in the HOSTS file on each client computer

   d. Create an A record on your DNS servers for NewAppServer1

2. You have resolved the issue. However, end users are complaining that NewAppServer1 is too complicated to enter every time they use their application. They have requested a shorter name to use with their application. What type of record would you create in order to meet this request?

   a. PTR

   b. MX

   c. SRV

   d. CNAME

   e. ALT

3. Which of the following records is used for specifying available mail servers for a domain?

   a. PTR

   b. MX

   c. SRV

   d. CNAME

   e. ALT

4. Which of the following records is used most often by reverse lookup zones for name resolution?

   a. PTR

   b. MX

   c. SRV

   d. CNAME

   e. ALT

5. Which of the following is not provided by SRV records?

   a. Location of services such as LDAP

   b. Network protocol information for available services

   c. Available mail servers for a domain

   d. Domain services information

MANAGING AND ADMINISTERING DNS IN WINDOWS SERVER 2008

Labs included in this chapter

- Lab 6.1 Adding a Server Core Domain Controller
- Lab 6.2 Designing a Windows Server 2008 Network
- Lab 6.3 Managing DNS with WinRM
- Lab 6.4 Research DNS Names and Records
- Lab 6.5 Restoring DNS Zones with Dnscmd

Microsoft MCTS Exam #70-642 Exam Objectives

Objective	Lab
Configure Name Resolution: Configure a Domain Name System (DNS) server	6.1, 6.2
Configure Name Resolution: Configure DNS zones	6.1, 6.2
Configure Name Resolution: Configure DNS records	
Configure Name Resolution: Configure DNS replication	6.2

Lab 6.1 Adding a Server Core Domain Controller

Objectives

The objective of this activity is to build a domain controller on a Windows Server 2008 Server Core computer.

Materials Required

This lab requires the following:

- The LABSCXX computer configured in previous activities
- The LABSRVXX computer configured in previous activities

Estimated completion time: **30 minutes**

Activity Background

In an Active Directory Directory Services environment, administrators will often install additional domain Controllers on a network for fault tolerance and spreading of workload. Server Core is an excellent choice for a domain controller, given the improved remote management capabilities of Windows Server 2008. This activity walks you through the process of installing an additional domain controller on a Server Core computer.

Activity

1. Log on to LABSRVXX.

2. Open a command prompt and enter **netsh int ip set dns "Internet Connection" static 127.0.0.1**.

3. Open Network Connections by typing **ncpa.cpl**.

4. Right-click **Internet Connection**, and then click **Properties**.

5. In the Internet Connection Properties dialog box, click **Internet Protocol Version 4 (TCP/IPv4)** and click **Properties**.

6. Click **Advanced**, click the **DNS** tab, and uncheck **Register this connection's addresses in DNS**. Click **OK** twice and then click **Close** to exit the adapter's properties.

7. Open the DNS console, expand the netlab.local folder, and delete any Host (A) records for LABSRVXX that are not using the IP address 192.168.1.201, if necessary. You should have only one if your server is currently connected to the Internet.

8. Stay logged on to LABSRVXX and log on to LABSCXX.

9. At the command prompt, enter **netdom join %computername% /domain:netlab.local /Userd: Administrator/passwordd:*** and enter **P@ssword** at the password prompt.

10. Enter **shutdown /r /t 0**.

11. Log on to LABSRVXX and open **Active Directory Users and Computers** from the Start > Administrative Tools menu.

12. In ADUC, expand the netlab.local domain and click the **Computers** container. Verify that LABSCXX is listed in the view pane as shown in Figure 6-1.

13. Click **LABSCXX**, click **Action** on the menu bar, click **Properties**, and then click the **Operating System** tab. Verify that Windows Server 2008 is listed as the name of the operating system. Click **OK** and log off LABSRVXX.

14. Log on to LABSCXX using the administrator@netlab.local domain account.

15. Enter **start /w ocsetup DNS-Server-Core-Role**.

16. When the command prompt is available, enter **oclist** and scroll through the results. Verify that DNS-Server-Core-Role is listed as an installed role.

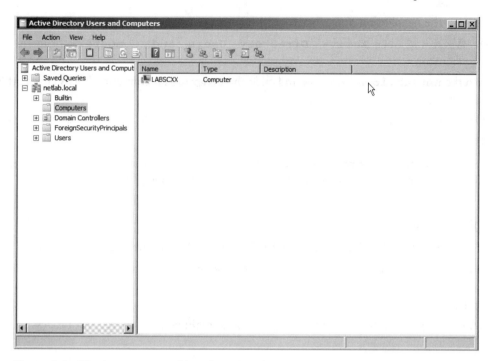

Figure 6-1 Viewing computer objects in Active Directory Users and Computers

17. Enter **DCpromo /?:promotion** and review the available switches for performing an unattended installation using DCpromo. Press any key when finished.

18. Enter **Dcpromo /unattend /replicaOrnewDomain:replica /replicaDomainDNSName:netlab. local /ConfirmGC:yes /UserDomain:netlab.local /username:administrator / Password:* /SafeModeAdminPassword:P@ssw0rd**. This will install the Active Directory Domain Services binaries and add LABSCXX as a domain controller for netlab.local, along with specifying the server as a Global Catalog server.

19. In the Windows Security window, enter **P@ssw0rd** and click **OK** as shown in Figure 6-2.

Figure 6-2 Credential prompt during DCpromo process

20. LABSCXX will finish the installation and reboot.

21. Log on to LABSRVXX and open **Active Directory Users and Computers** from the Start > Administrative Tools menu.

22. In ADUC, expand the **netlab.local** domain and click the **Computers** container. Verify that LABSCXX is not listed in the view pane.

23. Click the **Domain Controllers** organizational unit and verify that LABSCXX is listed in the view pane.

24. Log off LABSRVXX.

25. Log on to LABSCXX and enter **dnscmd /enumzones**. Verify that a primary zone has been created for netlab.local. This is due to DNS being installed prior to the running of DCpromo.

Certification Objectives

Objectives for MCTS Exam #70-642: Windows Server 2008 Network Infrastructure, Configuration:

- Configure Name Resolution: Configure a Domain Name System (DNS) server

Review Questions

1. Which of the following applications is used to complete the domain controller creation process?

   a. Netdom

   b. Netsh

   c. DCpromo

   d. Ocsetup

2. Which of the following utilities is used to add a computer into an Active Directory Domain?

   a. Netdom.exe

   b. Netsh

   c. DCpromo.msi

   d. DCpromo.exe

3. What type of replication is used between domain controllers in an Active Directory domain?

   a. Two-way

   b. Trusted

   c. Multi-master

   d. Single-master

4. True or False? Only Read-Only AD-integrated DNS zones can be created on Windows Server 2008 running Server Core.

5. Ocsetup _____ is the syntax for installing the DNS role on Windows Server 2008 running Server Core.

Lab 6.2 Designing a Windows Server 2008 Network

Objectives

The objective of this activity is to design and recommend a DNS implementation.

Materials Required

This lab requires the following:

- A pen or a pencil, and paper

Estimated completion time: 30 minutes

Activity Background

You have been hired as a consultant by Badger Widgets, Inc. They are a medium sized manufacturing firm whose network has grown over the last few years due to increased sales and business needs. Badger Widgets currently has three locations: Madison, Milwaukee, and Chicago. Each location has different infrastructure needs and service requirements as listed below:

- The Madison location is the central headquarters for Badger Widgets. They have a full IT staff along with an established network infrastructure that includes Windows Server 2008 servers and Windows Vista clients. Their IT staff needs to be able to manage the DNS zones for Madison and Milwaukee, along with the AD domains badgerwidgets.priv and mil.badgerwidgets.priv.

- The Milwaukee location is a satellite location used mainly for sales and distribution. However, the site requires name resolution for Internal and Internet-based hostnames. Also, they have a large number of clients who work out of their office so there are server's onsite to meet their needs. There is no IT Staff onsite so all management must be performed remotely.

- The Chicago location is a growing office for Badger Widgets. They have a large staff of employees in all areas of the company including IT Staff. The Chicago IT staff needs full management capabilities for their DNS zone records and their domain, chi.badgerwidgets.priv.

Activity

Based on the scenario above, answer the following questions:

1. Because each site will have at least two domain controllers, what type of zones will be deployed at each site? Include zone types and names.

2. What version and edition of Windows Server 2008 should be used at each site?

3. Draw a map of the DNS zones as they would map out after completion of this project.

Certification Objectives

Objectives for MCTS Exam #70-642: Windows Server 2008 Network Infrastructure, Configuration:

- Configure Name Resolution: Configure a Domain Name System (DNS) server
- Configure Name Resolution: Configure DNS replication
- Configure Name Resolution: Configure DNS zones

Review Questions

1. What type of domain controller is recommended for remote sites or branch offices which have no IT staff or poor security?

   a. Primary domain controller

   b. Backup domain controller

   c. Read-only domain controller

   d. Secure domain controller

2. What is the minimum number of DNS servers needed in an Active Directory environment?

   a. 1

   b. 2

   c. 3

   d. 4

3. What switch is used by Dnscmd to convert a standard DNS zone to an Active Directory–integrated zone?

   a. /ZoneChangetype

   b. /ZoneResetType

   c. /ZoneConvertType

   d. /ZoneReset

4. When using standard (file-based) DNS zones, how many primary servers can be authoritative for a domain?

   a. 1

   b. 2

   c. 3

   d. 4

5. What options are available for deploying read-only DNS zones?

   a. Create a primary zone and configure as read only on a DNS server

   b. Install secondary zone on a DNS server

   c. Install primary read-only zone on a standard domain controller

   d. Install AD-integrated zone and configure as read only on a domain controller

Lab 6.3 Managing DNS with WinRM

Objectives

The objective of this activity is to design and recommend a DNS implementation.

Materials Required

This lab requires the following:

- The LABSCXX computer configured in previous activities
- The LABSRVXX computer configured in previous activities

Estimated completion time: **30 minutes**

Activity Background

The Windows Remote Management, or WinRM, service implements the WS-Management protocol for remote management. WS-Management is a standard Web services protocol used for remote software and hardware management. The WinRM service utilizes a listener that waits for WS-Management requests. This listener needs to be configured using winrm.cmd command line tool or through Group Policy. One of the tools that work with WinRM is the Windows Remote Shell, or WinRS. With WinRS, administrators can run commands on a target server using a local command prompt.

Activity

1. Log on to LABSCXX.

2. At the command prompt, enter **winrm quickconfig** and enter **Y** when prompted, as shown in Figure 6-3. This configures Windows Remote Management (WinRM) for use on your server.

3. Enter **winrm enumerate winrm/config/listener**. You receive a response back displaying the currently running WinRM listener on your server.

4. Log on to LABSRVXX.

5. Open the command prompt, enter **winrm quickconfig**, and enter **Y** when prompted. This enables the WinRM listener on your server and enables the WinRM Firewall Exception.

6. Enter **winrm /?** and scroll through the WinRM help file.

7. Enter **winrs -?** and scroll through the winrs help file. Note the end of the file includes numerous examples for winrs.

8. Enter **winrs -r:labscxx ipconfig** to view the IP configuration on LABSCXX. Verify that the IP address listed is 192.168.1.202 on Ethernet adapter Netlab Network, as shown in Figure 6-4.

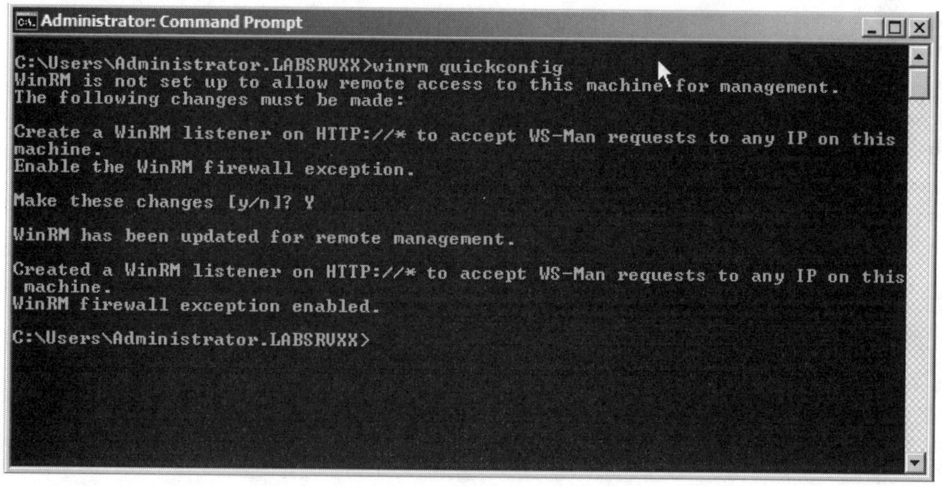

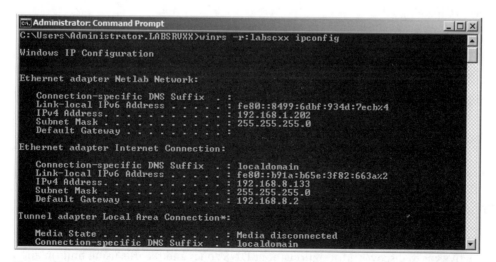

Figure 6-3   Configure Windows Remote Management for use

6

9. Enter **winrs -r:http://labscxx.netlab.local dnscmd /zoneadd WinRM.local /Primary /file winrm.local.dns**

10. Enter **winrs -r:http://labscxx.netlab.local dnscmd /enumzones** to verify the zone has been added on the remote server.

11. Enter **winrs -r:http://labscxx.netlab.local cmd.exe**

12. Enter **echo I am on %computername%** to display the name of the computer the command prompt is running on. It will display the server as your remote server, as shown in Figure 6-5. Note you do not need to use the **winrs -r** command because all commands are now being executed in the command prompt (cmd.exe) from the remote machine.

13. Enter **exit**.

Certification Objectives

Objectives for MCTS Exam #70-642: Windows Server 2008 Network Infrastructure, Configuration:

- Configure Name Resolution: Configure a Domain Name System (DNS) server
- Configure Name Resolution: Configure DNS replication
- Configure Name Resolution: Configure DNS zones

Figure 6-4   Viewing remote IP address configuration using WinRS

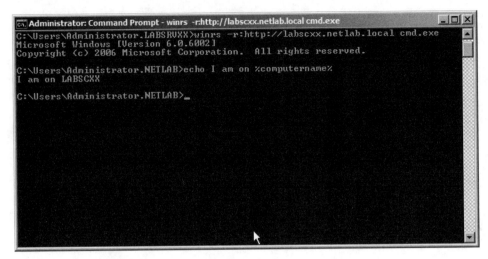

Figure 6-5   Viewing a remote server's name using WinRS

Review Questions

1. Which tools can be used to remotely configure a Windows Server 2008 DNS server? (Choose all that apply.)

   a. Server Manager

   b. DNScmd

   c. Servermanagercmd

   d. DNS Console

   e. WinRM

   f. Nslookup

2. What is the default port used by WinRM for the WinRM listener?

   a. 23

   b. 80

   c. 443

   d. 3389

3. Which command will execute the command ipconfig /all on a remote server, Server01, given a default installation of WinRM?

   a. Winrm -r:Server01 ipconfig /all

   b. Winrs -r:Server01 ipconfig /all

   c. Winrs Server01 -r ipconfig /all

   d. Winrm Server01 -r ipconfig /all

4. True or False? WinRM is installed by default and simply requires opening firewall ports for use.

5. Launching _____ through the Windows Remote Shell (WinRS) is an easier way to run multiple command line interface commands on a remote system.

Lab 6.4 Research DNS Names and Records

Objectives

The objective of this activity is to discover information about DNS zones and records using built-in and Internet-based tools.

Materials Required

This lab requires the following:

- Physical computer or virtual machine with Internet access and access to the nslookup command. This lab is designed to work in physical or virtual machine lab environments.

> Estimated completion time: **30 minutes**

Activity Background

One of the keys to success when troubleshooting a problem is gathering useful information. DNS is no exception to this. For DNS to work properly, zone records require correct configuration. For public DNS zones that you are not authoritative or responsible for, resolving issues can be difficult without the proper information. This is where tools such as Nslookup and www.networksolutions.com come in. Using these tools, you can view both DNS zone records and information about the zone such as administrative contacts and owner of record.

Activity

Using Nslookup and networksolutions.com, or other Internet domain Whois search tools, research the cengage.com domain name and record in the following information:

- Administrative contact address, phone number, and email address
- Expiration date of domain
- Listed name servers for domain
- Contact information for name server administrators
- Technical email contact
- Organization name and information
- IP address range assigned to domain
- Mail servers for domain including IP address
- IP address for www.cengage.com
- Start of authority record information for domain

Certification Objectives

Objectives for MCTS Exam #70-642: Windows Server 2008 Network Infrastructure, Configuration:

- Configure Name Resolution: Configure a Domain Name System (DNS) server

Review Questions

1. Whois information for a DNS zone would be helpful in discovering which of the following information about a public domain name? (Choose all that apply.)

    a. Owner of domain

    b. IP addresses used by domain

    c. Mail servers for domain

    d. Expiration date for domain

    e. All of the above

    f. None of the above

2. Which of the following commands will display the mail servers responsible for Microsoft.com?

    a. Nslookup -type=Mail Microsoft.com

    b. Nslookup -type=MX Microsoft.com

    c. Nslookup Microsoft.com -Mail

    d. Nslookup Microsoft.com -MX

    e. Nslookup /mailserverlookup Microsoft.com

3. Whois information for a DNS zone would be helpful in discovering which of the following information about a private domain name? (Choose all that apply.)

   a. Owner of domain

   b. IP addresses used by domain

   c. Mail servers for domain

   d. Expiration date for domain

   e. All of the above

   f. None of the above

4. True or False? By default, Nslookup will use the root hints on a local machine if another DNS IP address is not specified.

5. The _____ record includes information such as the responsible mail address, primary name server, and default TTL for a DNS zone.

Lab 6.5 Restoring DNS Zones with Dnscmd

Objectives

The objective of this activity is to perform backup and restore operations with Dnscmd.

Materials Required

This lab requires the following:

- The LABSCXX computer configured in previous activities

Estimated completion time: **45 minutes**

Activity Background

Dnscmd can be used to back up and restore a DNS zone and to create and modify DNS server information. This activity walks you through backing up and restoring a standard primary DNS zone. This process can be used to move a zone to another DNS server as well.

Activity

1. Log on to LABSCXX.

2. Enter **dnscmd /recordadd Winrm.local SRV1 A 192.168.200.10**.

3. Enter **dnscmd /recordadd Winrm.local SRV2 A 192.168.200.20**.

4. Enter **dnscmd /recordadd Winrm.local FTP CNAME SRV1.WINRM.LOCAL**

5. Enter **dnscmd /enumzones** and **dnscmd /zoneprint winrm.local**. Verify that all of the appropriate records above have been created and the zone is available.

6. Enter **dnscmd /zoneexport Winrm.local backup\Winrm.local.dns.bak**. This exports the Winrm zone to a backup file, as shown in Figure 6-6.

7. Enter **cd %systemroot%\system32\dns\backup** and then enter **dir** to view the contents of the backup directory.

8. Enter **dnscmd /zonedelete Winrm.local /f**

9. Enter **xcopy %systemroot%\system32\dns\backup\Winrm.local.dns.bak %systemroot%\system32\dns**. This copies the backed up file to the DNS directory where it can be read in during the zone creation in the next steps.

Figure 6-6   Exporting DNS zone with dnscmd /zoneexport

10. Enter **dnscmd /enumzones**.

11. Enter **dnscmd /zoneadd Winrm.local /primary /file Winrm.local.dns.bak /load** to restore the zone from the zone backup file, as shown in Figure 6-7.

12. Enter **nslookup ftp.winrm.local labscxx** to list the zone record for ftp.winrm.local and verify the zone is now available on LABSCXX.

13. Enter **dnscmd /enumzones**.

14. Enter **dnscmd /zoneprint Winrm.local** to verify all records have been restored for the DNS zone.

15. Log off LABSCXX.

Certification Objectives

Objectives for MCTS Exam #70-642: Windows Server 2008 Network Infrastructure, Configuration:

- Configure Name Resolution: Configure a Domain Name System (DNS) server
- Configure Name Resolution: Configure DNS zones
- Configure Name Resolution: Configure DNS records

Review Questions

1. What is the Dnscmd switch used for backing up a DNS zone file?

   a. /backupzone

   b. /exportzone

   c. /zoneexport

   d. /zonebackup

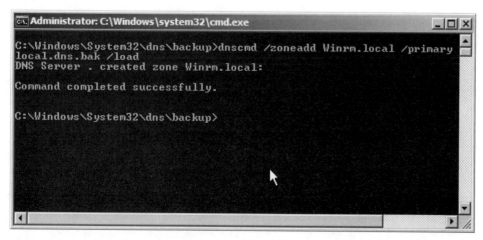

Figure 6-7   Restoring DNS zone from backup file

2. The DNS zone badgerwidgets.local has been deleted and needs to be restored from a backup. Backups of the zone file are located at c:\windows\system32\dns\backup, and the file is called badgerwidgets.local.dns.bak. Which of the following steps need to be completed in order to restore the zone? (Choose all that apply.)

   a. Enter dnscmd /zoneadd badgerwidgets.local /primary /file Winrm.local.dns.bak /load

   b. Enter dnscmd /zoneadd badgerwidgets.local /primary /file backup\Winrm.local.dns.bak /load

   c. Copy the backup file to c:\Windows\System32\dns

   d. Stop the DNS Server service

   e. Clear the DNS Server's cache

3. What is the dnscmd switch used to specify that a DNS zone should be created from an existing zone file?

   a. *DNSZoneFile* /create

   b. *DNSZoneFile* /import

   c. *DNSZoneFile* /load

   d. *DNSZoneFile* /zoneadd

4. Dnscmd _____ will display all of the zones available on a DNS server.

5. True or False? Canonical (CNAME), or Alias, provides an alias name for an IP address.

CHAPTER SEVEN

CONFIGURING FILE SERVICES IN WINDOWS SERVER 2008

Labs included in this chapter

- Lab 7.1 Backing Up Data with DFS Replication
- Lab 7.2 Troubleshooting DFS Replication
- Lab 7.3 Provisioning Shares with the Share and Storage Management Console
- Lab 7.4 Managing Files, Folders, and Shares from the Command Line

Microsoft MCTS Exam #70-642 Exam Objectives

Objective	Lab
Configure File and Print Services: Configure a file server	7.2, 7.3, 7.4
Configure File and Print Services: Configure distributed file system (DFS)	7.1, 7.2

Lab 7.1 Backing Up Data with DFS Replication

Objectives

The objective of this activity is to install and configure DFS Replication.

Materials Required

This lab requires the following:

- The LABSCXX computer configured in the previous activity
- The LABSRVXX computer configured in the previous activity
- This lab needs to be completed outside the hours of 12 a.m. to 6 p.m.

Estimated completion time: **45 minutes**

Activity Background

DFS Replication, or DFSR, is a role service of Windows Server 2008 that provides data replication capabilities between two or more servers. While often used in tandem with DFS Namespace, DFSR is an excellent choice by itself for backing up data from branch office sites to a central location. This allows administrators to remove the burden of site backups from branch office locations that often have no experienced IT personnel.

Activity

1. Log on to LABSCXX.
2. At the command prompt, enter **start /w ocsetup DFSN-Server**.
3. Enter **start /w ocsetup DFSR-Infrastructure-ServerEdition**.
4. Log on to LABSRVXX.
5. Open the command prompt and enter **servermanagercmd -i FS-DFS**. This installs the Distributed File System role, along with DFS Namespaces and DFS Replication.
6. Click **Start**, point to **Administrative Tools**, and click **DFS Management**.
7. In the Actions pane, click **New Replication Group**.
8. On the Replication Group Type screen, click **Multipurpose replication group** and click **Next**.
9. Type **DataBackup** as the name of the replication group, type **This group is used to collect data stores from remote servers for centralized offsite backup** in the description text box, and then click **Next**.
10. Click **Add** to open the Select Computers window for adding computers to the replication group.
11. Type **LABSCXX;LABSRVXX** in the text box and click **Check Names** to resolve the names. Click **OK**. A progress window opens while the chosen servers are verified.
12. When both servers are resolved, as shown in Figure 7-1, click **Next**.
13. Click **Next** to choose the default topology of Full Mesh.
14. Choose **Replicate during the specified days and times** and click **Edit Schedule**. This allows for the creation of a custom replication schedule.
15. In the Edit Schedule window, click and hold the cursor on the box in the upper left corner of the schedule grid. While keeping the left mouse button depressed, move the cursor downward at a 45 degree angle until you are in the square representing Saturday from 5-6 a.m., and then release the mouse button. The area selected is surrounded by a thick black line.
16. Choose **Full** from the Bandwidth usage drop-down box, as shown in Figure 7-2. The area selected turns royal blue, signifying that replication is allowed between the hours of 12 a.m. and 6 a.m. every day, and not allowed during the rest of the day. Click **OK** and then click **Next**.

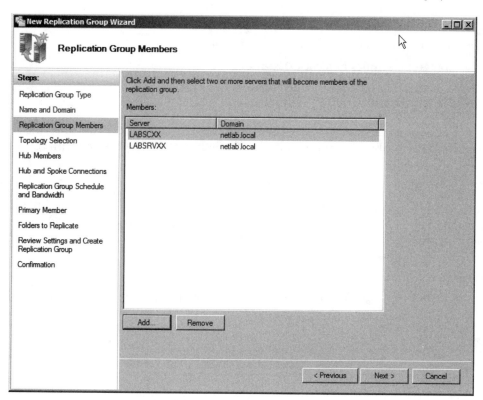

Figure 7-1 Adding DFS Replication group partners

17. On the Primary Member screen, choose **LABSCXX** as the primary member because it stores the changing data that needs to be backed up. Click **Next**.

18. On the Folders to Replicate screen, click **Add**, type **c:\DataBackup** for the local path of the folder to replicate, and click **OK**. Click **Yes** when asked to continue.

19. Click **Next**.

20. Click **Edit** to modify the local path of the replicated folder on LABSRVXX.

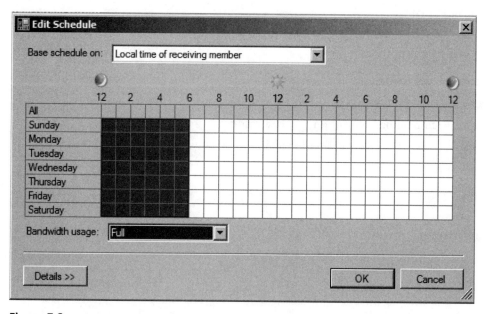

Figure 7-2 DFS Replication settings

21. Click **Enabled** and enter **c:\RemoteBackup\LABSCXX\DataBackup** as the local path.

22. Click **OK** and, when prompted, click **Yes.** Click **Next** to continue.

23. Review the Replication group settings and click **Create**.

24. Click **Close**. The Replication Delay message box appears. Click **OK**.

25. Log on to LABSCXX.

26. Enter **xcopy c:\windows\en-us*.* c:\DataBackup** to copy some data into the replicated folder location created previously. Wait approximately 15 minutes before proceeding with the rest of this activity.

27. Switch back to LABSRVXX.

28. In Windows Explorer, browse to **c:\RemoteBackup\LABSCXX**. Note that the folder named **DataBackup** exists, but it is empty. This is because the creation of the replication group occurred outside of the established replication window.

29. Log off LABSRVXX and LABSCXX.

The results of the above steps will only occur if the lab steps were completed outside of the 12 a.m. to 6 a.m. time range.

Certification Objectives

Objectives for MCTS Exam #70-642: Windows Server 2008 Network Infrastructure, Configuration:

- Configuring File and Print Services: Configure Distributed File System (DFS)

Review Questions

1. Which of the following commands can be used to install only the DFS Replication role service on a computer running the Full edition of Windows Server 2008?

    a. servermanagercmd –i FS-DFS-R

    b. servermanagercmd –i FS-DFS-Replication

    c. servermanagercmd –i DFSR-Infrastructure-ServerEdition

    d. servermanagercmd –i DFSR

2. Which of the following is not a possible usage of DFS Replication?

    a. Load balancing data between servers

    b. Backing up data from a remote site

    c. Providing fault-tolerant data resources

    d. Creating a centralized naming convention for data resources

3. Which of the following uses DFS Replication for maintaining consistent data?

    a. NETLOGON share

    b. SYSVOL share

    c. Printer sharing

    d. AD DS site information

4. Ocsetup _____ will install DFS Replication role services on Windows Server 2008 running Server Core.

5. True or False? DFS Replication schedules can only be set by day and not by time of day.

Lab 7.2 Troubleshooting DFS Replication

Objectives

The objective of this activity is to use command-line tools for managing and troubleshooting DFS Replication.

Materials Required

This lab requires the following:

- The LABSCXX computer configured in the previous activity
- The LABSRVXX computer configured in the previous activity
- This lab needs to be completed within one hour of completing Lab 7-1, and outside the hours of 12 a.m. to 6 p.m.

Estimated completion time: **45 minutes**

Activity Background

DFS Replication will automatically replicate itself based on the schedule set by an administrator. However, there may be occasions when replication does not occur or replication needs to be initiated outside of the replication window. Using tools like Event Viewer, Dfsrdiag, and Dfsradmin, administrators can research DFS Replication events to find errors, then use tools to resolve any issues discovered. Dfsrdiag is a command-line tool for running diagnostic tests on DFS Replication. Along with diagnostic testing, it can be used to sync replication partners and poll Active Directory for configuration/replication changes. Dfsradmin can be used to administrate DFS Replication from the command line by adding to and modifying DFS Replication settings.

Activity

1. Log on to LABSRVXX.

2. In Windows Explorer, browse to `c:\RemoteBackup\LABSCXX\DataBackup`. Note that the folder is empty because replication has still not taken place.

3. Open Event Viewer from Administrative Tools and expand **Applications and Services Logs** to view the **DFS Replication** events.

4. Double-click the top event warning with an Event ID of 4102. This displays the Event Properties window shown in Figure 7-3.

5. Review the event information. This event tells you that LABSRVXX is waiting to perform the initial replication of the DataBackup folder to be located at c:\LABSCXX\DataBackup. Again, this is due to the creation of the replicated folder outside of the replication window.

6. Click **Close** and minimize Event Viewer.

7. Open the command prompt and enter **dfsrdiag /?** to display the usage information for Dfsrdiag.

8. Enter **dfsrdiag pollad** to force LABSRVXX to contact Active Directory and check for any changes to replication or configuration settings.

9. Enter **dfsrdiag backlog /rgname:DataBackup /rfname:DataBackup /smem:LABSCXX /rmem:LABSRVXX**. This displays the backlog of files waiting to be replicated from LABSCXX to LABSRVXX. Note the four files waiting for replication as shown in Figure 7-4.

10. Enter **dfsradmin conn list schedule /rgname:DataBackup /sendmem:LABSCXX /recvmem: LABSRVXX** to display the replication schedule for the DataBackup replication group.

11. Enter **dfsrdiag syncnow /partner:LABSCXX /rgname:DataBackup /time:1**. This forces synchronization of replication folders by changing the current replication mode to Replicate Now for one minute.

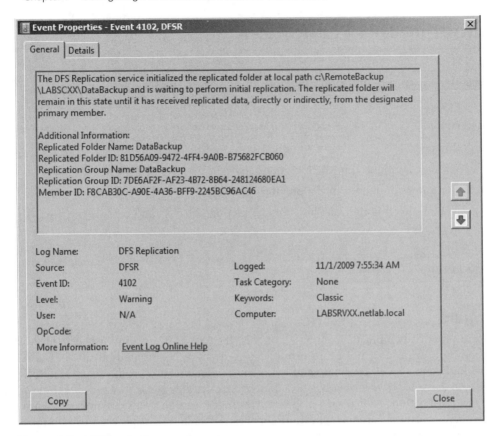

Figure 7-3   DFS Replication event warning

12. Repeat the command you entered in Step 9. This time you receive a message that no backlog exists.

13. Enter **dir c:\RemoteBackup\LABSCXX\DataBackup** to list the contents of the replication folder on LABSRVXX. Four files are now listed.

14. Return to Event Viewer, click **Refresh** on the Action menu, and review the three new informational messages listed under DFS Replication. Note the older Event ID 5106 that was triggered by Step 11 above signifying the replication mode change, and Event ID 4104 signifying the successful replication of data from LABSCXX.

15. Return to the command prompt and enter **dfsradmin /?** to list the commands available for Dfsradmin.

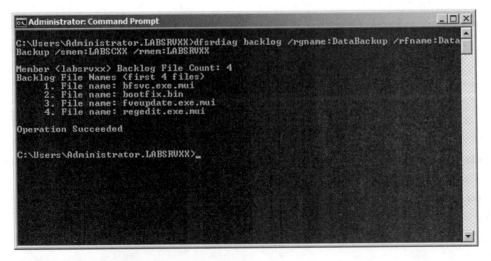

Figure 7-4   Viewing DFS Replication backlog

Figure 7-5   Viewing DFS Replication schedule with Dfsradmin

16. Enter **dfsradmin conn set sched full /rgname:DataBackup /sendmem:LABSCXX /recvmem:LABSRVXX** to set the replication schedule to full replication. This is equal to replication 24 hours/day and seven days/week.

17. Enter **dfsradmin conn list schedule /rgname:DataBackup /sendmem:LABSCXX /recvmem:LABSRVXX** to show that the schedule has changed to full replication, as shown in Figure 7-5. Note the use of **ffff** to represent full replication in each hour slot.

18. Enter **xcopy c:\Windows*.exe c:\RemoteBackup\LABSCXX\DataBackup** and log off LABSRVXX.

19. Log on to LABSCXX and enter **dfsradmin conn set sched full /rgname:DataBackup /sendmem:LABSRVXX /recvmem:LABSCXX** to set the replication schedule to full replication.

20. Wait approximately 5-10 minutes and enter **dfsrdiag backlog /rgname:DataBackup /rfname:DataBackup /smem:LABSRVXX /rmem:LABSCXX**. You should receive a message that no backlog exists. If files are listed in the backlog, repeat this step every minute until no files are listed.

21. Enter **dir c:\DataBackup**. You should see 12 files listed, including eight ending in an EXE extension.

22. Log off LABSCXX.

Certification Objectives

Objectives for MCTS Exam #70-642: Windows Server 2008 Network Infrastructure, Configuration:

• Configuring File and Print Services: Configure Distributed File System (DFS)

Review Questions

1. Which of the following commands can be used to view the status of files to be replicated between DFS Replication partners?

   a. dfsrdiag /testdfsintegrity

   b. dfsrdiag SyncNow

   c. dfsrdiag Backlog

   d. dfsrdiag PollAD

2. Which of the following commands is used to manually sync a DFS Replication target?

   a. dfsrdiag /testdfsintegrity

   b. dfsrdiag SyncNow

   c. dfsrdiag Backlog

   d. dfsrdiag PollAD

3. Which of the following commands is used to force synchronization of DFS Replication and configuration settings?

    a. dfsrdiag /testdfsintegrity

    b. dfsrdiag SyncNow

    c. dfsrdiag Backlog

    d. dfsrdiag PollAD

4. Which of the following commands is used to modify DFS Replication settings?

    a. dfsrdiag

    b. dfsutil

    c. dfscfg

    d. dfsradmin

5. True or False? Creation of a DFS namespace is required to initiate replication between DFS Replication partners.

Lab 7.3 Provisioning Shares with the Share and Storage Management Console

Objectives

The objective of this activity is to provision storage and shared folder resources through the Share and Storage Management console.

Materials Required

This lab requires the following:

- The LABSCXX computer configured in previous activities
- The LABSRVXX computer configured in previous activities

Estimated completion time: **30 minutes**

Activity Background

Windows Server 2008 provides a new tool for managing storage and file shares. It is called the Share and Storage Management console. From within the console, administrators can view the current shares and volumes for a local or remote server. With the built-in wizards, administrators can not only create new disk volumes or file shares; they can also create new shares and provision the shares to use services like DFS in a single process. This can help streamline processes that could require the use of multiple consoles and menus without the Share and Storage Management console. Additionally, administrators can manage open files and sessions for shares just like the Shared Folder snap-in.

Activity

1. Log on to LABSRVXX.

2. Click **Start**, point to **Administrative Tools**, and click **Share and Storage Management**.

3. Click **Action** on the menu bar and click **Provision Storage**.

4. Click **Next** twice to get to the Volume Size screen. Enter **5.0 GB** as the new volume size and click **Next**.

5. Click **Next** to accept the default selection of the E: drive for the volume.

6. Enter **Data** as the volume label, click **Next**, and click **Create** to complete the storage provisioning process.

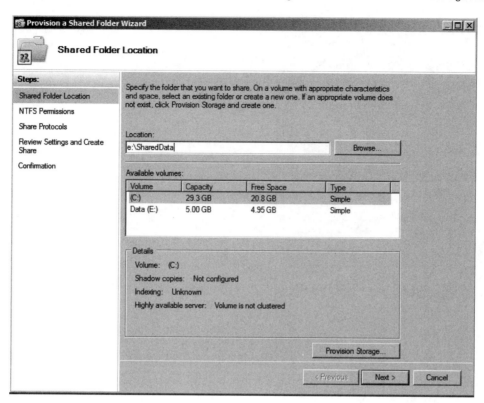

Figure 7-6 Shared Folder Location screen

7. If you receive a warning that you need to format the disk, click **Cancel** because the disk is formatted as part of the Provision Storage Wizard.

8. Check the **After closing the wizard, run the share provisioning wizard to create a share** check box and click **Close** to launch the Shared Folder wizard.

9. On the Shared Folder Location screen, enter **e:\SharedData**, as shown in Figure 7-6, and click **Next**. When prompted to create the location, click **Yes**.

10. Click **Next** to choose the default NTFS permissions.

11. Click **Next** to accept the default share name of SharedData.

12. In the Description text box, enter **This folder contains shared documents for use by all users.**

13. Click the **Advanced** button, select **Allow this number of users**, and enter **1**. Click **OK** and **Next** to continue.

14. Click the option button for **Administrators have Full Control; all other users and groups have only Read access**, and click **Next** to continue.

15. Click **Next** to bypass publishing the share to a DFS namespace.

16. Review the share folder settings and click **Create**. Click **Close** when the share creation is complete.

17. Click the **Shares** tab and double-click **SharedData** in the Shares pane.

18. Review the properties for **SharedData**, as shown in Figure 7-7, and click **Cancel**.

19. Close the Share and Storage Management console.

Certification Objectives

Objectives for MCTS Exam #70-642: Windows Server 2008 Network Infrastructure, Configuration:

• Configuring IP Addressing and Services: Configure a File Server

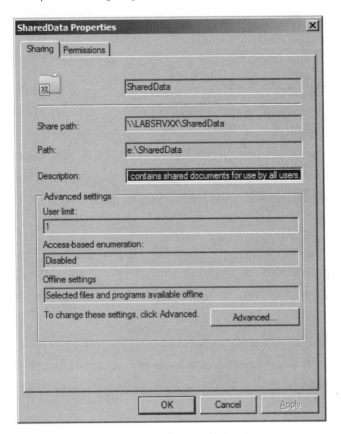

Figure 7-7 Properties of SharedData folder share

Review Questions

1. Which of the following tools can be directly used for creating Shared folder resources? (Choose all that apply.)

   a. Windows Explorer

   b. Net share

   c. Net use

   d. Share and Storage Management console

   e. Disk Management

2. What are the default share permissions when creating a shared folder resource?

   a. Everyone: Full Control

   b. Everyone: Read; Administrators: Change

   c. Authenticated Users: Read

   d. Everyone: Read

3. What is the cumulative impact on access to a share folder's contents when combining NTFS/user level and shared permissions?

   a. The least restrictive permissions apply

   b. The NTFS permissions override the shared permissions

   c. The most restrictive permissions apply

   d. The shared permissions override the NTFS permissions

4. The _____ console is used to manage shared folders along with disk storage on a Windows Server 2008 computer.

5. True or False? Inherited permissions override all explicit permissions applied at the file or folder level.

Lab 7.4 Managing Files, Folders, and Shares from the Command Line

Objectives

The objective of this lab is to manage files, folders, and shares through the use of built-in command line utilities.

Materials Required

This lab requires the following:

- The LABSRVXX computer configured in previous activities

Estimated completion time: **30 minutes**

Activity Background

Windows Server 2008 provides a number of command-line utilities for managing files, folders, and shared resources. Tools like Icacls, Takeown, and Net share can be used by administrators to work with file resources quickly from the command line or can be used for automated processes through batch scripts.

Activity

1. Log on to LABSRVXX.

2. Open a command prompt and enter **dir** to list the contents of the current directory.

3. Enter **cd c:**. This command, cd, stands for change directory and allows you to move between locations in the directory by simply typing in the path.

4. Enter **dir** and review the contents of c:\.

5. Enter **md DataFolder**. The make directory, or md, command allows you to create a folder to build out a directory structure. If the exact path is omitted as in this step, the folder is created in the current location of the command prompt, which is c:\.

6. Enter **md c:\Directory1\Folder1\Subfolder1**. Since a directory path was included, this will create the directory structure from the command.

7. Enter **icacls /? | More** to view the usage of the Icacls utility. Click the space bar to continue scrolling through the list. Icacls is a command line utility for administering the Access Control Lists for files and folders on a Windows Server 2008 computer.

8. Enter **icacls /? > icacls.txt**. This sends the output of the Icacls help command into a text file for easier reading.

9. Enter **icacls.txt** to view the text file in Notepad. Review the Icacls help file and close the file when finished.

10. Enter **icacls c:\Directory1** to display the Access Control List, or ACL, for a folder, as shown in Figure 7-8.

11. Enter **icacls Directory1 /Inheritance:r**. This will stop the inheritance of permissions and will remove all inherited Access Control Entries (ACEs).

12. Enter **icacls Directory1 /Deny Users:F**. This denies the Users group Full control access to the folder to simulate being locked out of a folder directory.

13. Enter **cd directory1**. You will receive an "Access is denied." response due to the Deny permission applied above.

14. Enter **takeown /?** to view the syntax of the Takeown command. Takeown, short for take ownership, is a command line utility that administrators can use to modify file ownership, even when denied access. It is used in tandem with Icacls to restore directory access for users and groups.

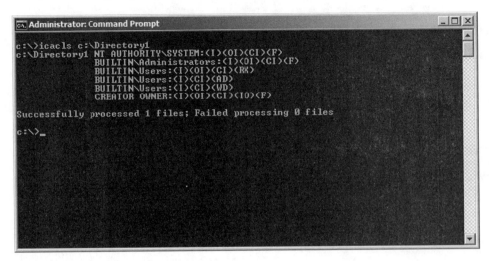

Figure 7-8 Displaying folder permissions with icacls

15. Enter **takeown /F Directory1**. This makes the currently logged-on account owner of the folder, as shown in Figure 7-9.

16. Enter **icacls Directory1 /reset**. This resets permissions back to the default permissions inherited from the parent drive, c:\.

17. Enter **icacls Directory1**. You should see that the default permissions have been restored and the Users group is no longer denied full control.

18. Enter **cd Directory1** to verify you can now access the directory.

19. Enter **net share /?** to view the syntax of the net share command. Net share is a command-line utility for managing file shares in Windows Server 2008.

20. Enter **net share** to view all of the shares available on LABSRVXX.

21. Enter **net share Directory1=c:\Directory1 /Grant:Administrators,Read /Remark:"This is a share created from the command line"** to create a new file share, set the permissions, and add a description of the share.

22. Log off LABSRVXX.

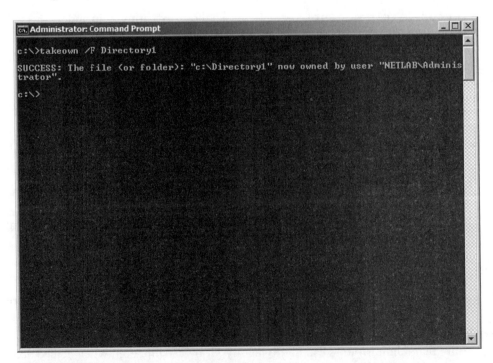

Figure 7-9 Using takeown to change folder ownership

Certification Objectives

Objectives for MCTS Exam #70-642: Windows Server 2008 Network Infrastructure, Configuration:

- Configuring IP Addressing and Services: Configure a file server

Review Questions

1. Which of the following commands can be used to view the ACL for a file or folder? (Choose all that apply.)

   a. icacls

   b. takeown

   c. net share

   d. cacls

2. You are an administrator for a small company and have received a request to make some changes to a folder directory, e:\MarketingData. When you attempt to view the permissions of the directory to make changes, you are denied access. Which of the following commands are needed to gain access to the folder and restore the default inherited permissions?

   a. takeown /F e:\MarketingData

   b. takeown e:\MarketingData

   c. icacls /F e:\MarketingData /ResetInheritance

   d. net own /F e:\MarketingData

   e. icacls e:\MarketingData /inheritance:r

3. Which of the following commands is used to display shared folder resources on a computer?

   a. icacls

   b. takeown

   c. net share

   d. net use

4. What switch is used with the Takeown command to connect with a remote Windows Server 2008 computer?

   a. /C

   b. /R

   c. /S

   d. /D

5. True or False? It is not possible to modify folder and file permissions to prevent access by the administrators group permanently.

Introduction to Printers in a Windows Server 2008 Network

Labs included in this chapter

- Lab 8.1 Installing the Print Services Role and Creating Printers

- Lab 8.2 Managing Print Servers in Windows Server 2008

- Lab 8.3 Deploying Printers with Group Policy

Microsoft MCTS Exam #70-642 Exam Objectives

Objective	Lab
Configure File and Print Services: Configure and monitor Print Services	8.1, 8.2, 8.3

Lab 8.1 Installing the Print Services Role and Creating Printers

Objectives

The objective of this activity is to install the Print Services role and create printers.

Materials Required

This lab requires the following:

- The LABSCXX computer configured in previous activities
- The LABSRVXX computer configured in previous activities

Estimated completion time: **30 minutes**

Activity Background

The Print Services role in Active Directory allows administrators to share printers and to centrally manage network printers and print servers. New to Windows Server 2008 is the ability to deploy printer connections via Group Policy. In this lab, you install the Print Services role, add a print server, and install a shared printer.

Activity

1. Log on to LABSCXX.

2. At the command prompt, enter **netsh firewall set service fileandprint enable** to allow file and print management on LABSCXX. Once the firewall is changed, enter **start /w ocsetup Printing-ServerCore-Role**. This installs the Print Services role and the Print Server role service.

3. If the Windows Package Manager message box opens, requesting a restart, click **Yes.**

4. After your computer restarts, log on to LABSRVXX.

5. Open a command prompt and enter **servermanagercmd.exe -install Print-Server** to install the Print Services role and the Print Server role service, if these components are not already installed. The Print Server role service is the only required role service for installing the Print Services role.

6. Enter **servermanagercmd.exe -install Print-Internet**. This installs Internet Printing functionality on a Windows Server 2008 print server.

7. Click **Start**, point to **Administrative Tools**, and then click **Print Management**.

8. Expand **Print Servers** and verify that LABSRVXX is displayed in the listing.

9. Click **Print Servers** in the left pane, click **Action** on the menu bar, and then click **Add/Remove Servers**. Enter **LABSCXX** in the Add servers text box and click **Add to List**, as shown in Figure 8-1. Click **OK** to close the Add/Remove Servers dialog box.

10. Expand **LABSCXX** in the left pane, click **Printers**, click **Action** on the menu bar, and click **Add Printer**.

11. Click **Add a new printer using an existing port** and then make sure **LPT1: (Printer Port)** is selected. Click **Next**.

12. Click **Install a new driver** and click **Next**. Choose **Generic/Text Only** from under the **Generic** manufacturer listing and then click **Next**.

13. In the Printer Name and Sharing Settings dialog box, type **PrinterSC01** as the printer name and the share name and specify **LABSCXX** as the location, as shown in Figure 8-2. Click **Next** to continue.

14. In the Printer Found dialog box, click **Next** to continue.

15. On the Completing the Network Printer Installation Wizard page, click **Finish**.

16. Expand **LABSRVXX** in the left pane (if necessary), click **Printers**, click **Action** on the menu bar, and click **Add Printer**.

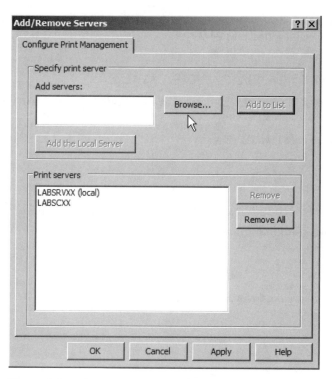

Figure 8-1   Adding a print server to the Print Management console

17. Click **Add a new printer using an existing port** and then make sure **LPT1: (Printer Port)** is selected. Click **Next**.

18. Click **Use an existing printer driver on the computer**, click **Generic/Text Only**, and then click **Next**. (If no printers have been installed on the computer, click **Install a new driver**, and then click **Generic/Text Only**.)

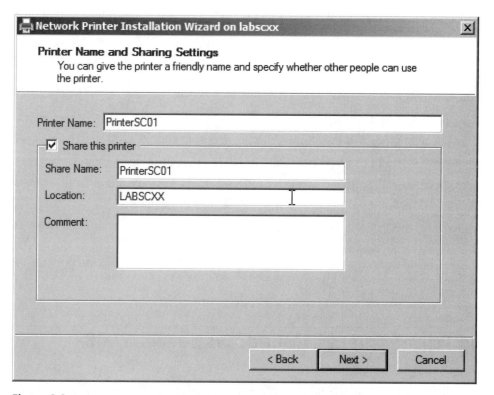

Figure 8-2   Sharing a printer in the Add Printer Wizard

19. In the Printer Name and Sharing Settings dialog box, type **Printer02** as the printer name and the share name and specify **LABSRVXX** as the location. Click **Next** to continue.

20. In the Printer Found dialog box, click **Next** to continue.

21. On the Completing the Network Printer Installation Wizard page, click **Finish**.

22. Verify that the new printer appears in the PMC by clicking the **Printers** node below LABSRVXX and LABSCXX in the left pane.

23. Close the Print Management Console and log off LABSRVXX.

Certification Objectives

Objectives for MCTS Exam #70-642: Windows Server 2008 Network Infrastructure, Configuration:

- Configure File and Print Services: Configure and monitor Print Services

Review Questions

1. Which of the following cannot be used for installing Print Services in Windows Server 2008?

    a. Servermanagercmd

    b. Add Roles Wizard

    c. Ocsetup

    d. PowerShell 1.0

2. Which of the following role services are not required to install the Print Services role? (Choose all that apply.)

    a. LPR Port Monitor

    b. Print Server

    c. Internet Printing

    d. LPD Service

3. Which of the following role services provides UNIX-based computers access to printers shared on Windows Server 2008?

    a. LPR Port Monitor

    b. Print Server

    c. Internet Printing

    d. LPD Service

4. Which of the following commands will install the Print Services role and all associated role services?

    a. servermanagercmd.exe –install Print-Services LPD-Service Internet-Printing

    b. servermanagercmd.exe –install Print-Services Print-LPD-Service Internet-Printing

    c. servermanagercmd.exe –install Print-Services Print-LPD-Service Print-Internet

    d. servermanagercmd.exe –install Print-Services-Full

5. True or False? To create a shared printer, the printer must be shared during the printer creation using Add Printer Wizard.

Lab 8.2 Managing Print Servers in Windows Server 2008

Objectives

The objective of this activity is to use various built-in Windows Server 2008 administrative tools for management of remote and local print servers.

Materials Required

This lab requires the following:

- The LABSCXX computer configured in previous activities
- The LABSRVXX computer configured in previous activities

> Estimated completion time: **30 minutes**

Activity Background

Windows Server 2008 includes a number of useful command-line utilities for working with print servers including Prnmngr.vbs and Prnjobs. Using the command line is an excellent alternative to the GUI, especially when working with Server Core or using Windows Remote Shell (WinRS).

Activity

1. Log on to LABSRVXX.

2. At a command prompt, type **cd %systemroot%\system32\printing_admin_scripts\en-us** and then press **Enter** to change to the Printing Scripts directory.

3. Enter **cscript //H:Cscript //S**. This sets cscript as the default scripting host.

4. Enter **prnmngr** to view the options and syntax for the utility.

5. Enter **prnmngr -l** (lowercase l) to display the printers on the server, as shown in Figure 8-3.

6. Enter **prnmngr -a -p "Printer03" -m "Generic / Text Only" -r "Lpt2:"**. This command adds a local printer, Printer03, to LABSRVXX, using LPT2 and the "Generic / Text Only" driver.

7. Enter **prnmngr -l -s LABSCXX** to display the printers on LABSCXX.

8. Enter **Notepad** to launch Notepad, and type **This is a test print job**. This simulates a print job.

9. From the File menu, click **Print** to launch the Print menu. Select Printer03 from the menu and click **Print**. This sends a print job to Printer03. Since Printer03 is not connected to a real print device, it will go into Error-Printing status.

Figure 8-3 Displaying local printers with prnmngr.vbs

Figure 8-4   Viewing active print jobs with prnmngr.vbs

10. Close Notepad and enter **prnjobs -l -p "Printer03"** at the command prompt. This allows you to use the Prnjobs utility to list the current print jobs on Printer03, as shown in Figure 8-4. Record the Job ID for the print job as listed in the command output:_____

11. Using the Job ID from the previous step, enter **prnjobs -m -p "Printer02" -j XX** where XX is the Job ID you recorded in Step 10. The -m switch allows you to resume the print job.

12. Enter **prnjobs -x -p "Printer03" -j XX** to cancel the print job on Printer02. Cancelled print jobs can take a few minutes to clear. Wait 2-3 minutes before proceeding to the next step.

13. Enter **prnmngr -d -p "Printer03"** to delete Printer03 without confirmation.

14. Enter **net stop "Print Spooler"** to stop the Print Spooler service. Printer issues can often be resolved by simply restarting the Print Spooler service on a print server.

15. Enter **net start "Print Spooler"** to start the Print Spooler service again.

16. Enter **Exit** to close the command prompt window.

17. Open the Powershell 1.0 shell and enter **Restart-Service -displayname "Print Spooler"**. Using the Restart-Service cmdlet is another option for restarting.

18. Log off LABSRXX.

Certification Objectives

Objectives for MCTS Exam #70-642: Windows Server 2008 Network Infrastructure, Configuration:

• Configure File and Print Services: Configure and monitor Print Services

Review Questions

1. Which of the following Prnmgr.vbs switches will display all of the printers configured on a local computer?

    a. -a

    b. -l

    c. -list

    d. -p

2. Which of the following commands will display the current print jobs on a printer named Office Printer 01?

   a. cscript prnjobs.vbs -l "Office Printer 01"

   b. cscript prnjobs.vbs -p "Office Printer 01"

   c. cscript prnmngr.vbs -l -p "Office Printer 01"

   d. cscript prnjobs.vbs -l -p "Office Printer 01"

3. Prnmgr and Prnjobs.vbs both require the following to run on Windows Server 2008?

   a. PowerShell 1.0

   b. Window Management Instrumentation

   c. Windows Scripting Host

   d. Windows Installer Service

4. True or False? Prnjobs is used to add and delete printers from the command line.

5. _____ is the PowerShell cmdlet for recycling a service such as the Print Spooler service.

Lab 8.3 Deploying Printers with Group Policy

Objectives

The objective of this activity is to deploy network printers to clients using Group Policy in Windows Server 2008.

Materials Required

This lab requires the following:

- The LABSCXX computer configured in previous activities
- The LABSRVXX computer configured in previous activities

Estimated completion time: **30 minutes**

Activity Background

The ability to deploy printers within an Active Directory domain using Group Policy is a welcome addition to Windows Server 2008. This provides administrators with great flexibility and control over deploying printers, not to mention easing the burden of walking users through printer installations.

Activity

1. Log on to LABSRVXX.

2. Click **Start**, point to **Administrative Tools**, and then click **Group Policy Management** to open the Group Policy Management Console (GPMC).

3. Expand the forest and domain nodes until you can click **Domain Controllers** as shown in Figure 8-5.

4. Click **Action** on the menu bar and click **Create a GPO in this domain, and Link it here**.

5. In the **New GPO** window, type **DeployPrinterCompGPO** as the name and click **OK**.

6. Close the GPMC.

7. Open the Print Management console.

8. Expand the nodes until you reach PrinterSC01 on LABSCXX. Click **PrinterSC01**.

9. Click **Action** on the menu bar and click **Deploy with Group Policy** to launch the Deploy with Group Policy window.

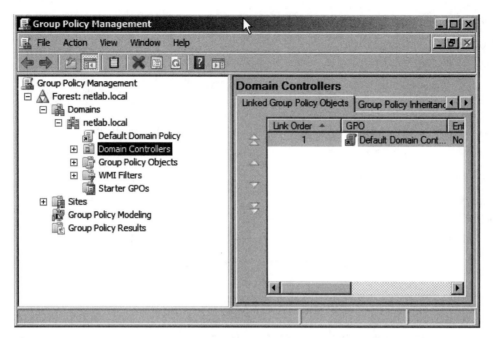

Figure 8-5   Using the Group Policy Management Console

10. Click **Browse** and double-click **Domain Controllers.netlab.local** to view the Group Policy Objects located under the Domain Controllers OU.

11. Click **DeployPrinterCompGPO** and click **OK**.

12. Place a check mark next to **The computers that this GPO applies to (per machine)** and click **Add**. This adds the GPO to the listing, as shown in Figure 8-6.

13. Click **OK** three times to deploy the GPO.

14. Open a command prompt and enter **gpupdate**. This forces the update of the Group Policy client service on LABSRVXX.

15. Open the **Printers** window from Control Panel to verify that PrinterSC01 was deployed, as shown in Figure 8-7 (in Large Icons view).

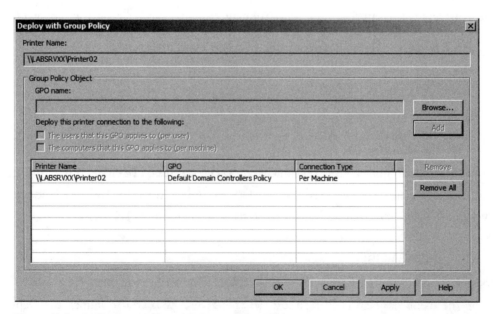

Figure 8-6   Deploying printers with Group Policy Objects

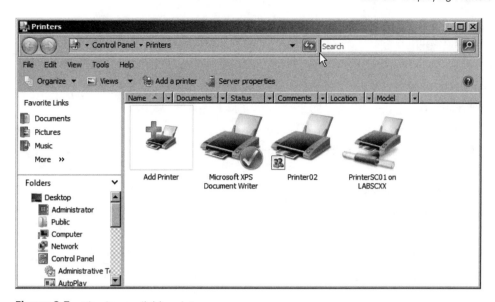

Figure 8-7 Viewing available printers

16. Open the GPMC, expand Domain Controllers in the left pane (if necessary), and double-click **DeployPrinterCompGPO**. Click **OK** if you receive a message about connecting to a link for a GPO.

17. Click **Action** on the menu bar and click **Link Enabled** to remove the check mark signifying the GPO is enabled. Disabling the GPO means that its settings no longer apply to any objects it currently applies to.

18. Open a command prompt and enter **gpupdate**.

19. Open the Printers icon in Control Panel to verify that PrinterSC01 is no longer deployed.

Deployment of printers with group policy is supported on Windows 7, Windows Server 2008, and Windows Server 2008 R2 clients with the installation of additional software. For prior clients, administrators need to download and deploy the PushPrinterConnections.exe tool. For more information about this tool and deploying printers with Group Policy, visit technet.microsoft.com and search for **Deploying Printers by Using Group Policy**.

Certification Objectives

Objectives for MCTS Exam #70-642: Windows Server 2008 Network Infrastructure, Configuration:

- Configure File and Print Services: Configure and monitor Print Services

Review Questions

1. Which of the following tools is used to create Group Policy Objects for deploying printers in Windows Server 2008?

   a. Group Policy Management Console

   b. Active Directory Users and Computers

   c. gpupdate

   d. Printer Management console

2. Which of the following tools is used to add printers to Group Policy Objects for deploying in Windows Server 2008?

   a. Group Policy Management Console

   b. Active Directory Users and Computers

   c. gpupdate

   d. Printer Management console

3. Which of the following is required for deploying printers to Windows XP clients, but not Windows 7 Clients? (Choose all that apply.)

   a. Group Policy Management Console

   b. Pushprinterconnections.exe

   c. Group Policy Preferences

   d. Printer Management console

4. Which of the following tools is used to create Group Policy Objects for deploying printers in Windows Server 2008?

   a. Group Policy Management Console

   b. Active Directory Users and Computers

   c. gpupdate

   d. Printer Management console

5. By typing _____ at a command prompt, administrators can manually initiate the update of the Group Policy client service.

NETWORK POLICY AND ACCESS SERVICES IN WINDOWS SERVER 2008

Labs included in this chapter

- Lab 9.1 Installing and Configuring Routing and Remote Access (RRAS)
- Lab 9.2 Implementing a PPTP Virtual Private Network (VPN)
- Lab 9.3 Configuring a Network Policy for Remote Access Users

Microsoft MCTS Exam #70-642 Objectives

Objective	Lab
Configuring Network Access: Configure remote access	9.1, 9.2, 9.3

Lab 9.1 Installing and Configuring Routing and Remote Access (RRAS)

Objective

The objective of this activity is to install and configure Routing and Remote Access in Windows Server 2008.

Materials Required

This lab requires the following:

- The LABSRVXX computer configured in previous activities
- An additional Full installation of Windows Server 2008 computer, named LABSRV1XX, with one network adapter connected to the private network used by LABSRVXX

Estimated completion time: **30 minutes**

Activity Background

As with other roles, Windows Server 2008 does not install Routing and Remote Access by default. This means that administrators must install and configure RRAS prior to using it. Although RRAS can be configured as both a router and as a provider of remote access services, this activity focuses on remote access only.

Activity

1. Log on to LABSRVXX as Administrator.
2. In Server Manager, start the Add Roles wizard. If the Before You Begin screen appears, click **Next** to access the Select Server Roles screen.
3. Click the **Network Policy and Access Services** check box to select it and click **Next** twice.
4. On the Select Role Services screen, click the **Routing and Remote Access Services** check box and click **Next**. This will install the Remote Access Service and Routing services.
5. Click **Install** to begin the installation process, which will take a few minutes.
6. Once the installation is complete, click **Close**.
7. Open Server Manager and expand the **Network Policy and Access Services** node to view the Routing and Remote Access node.
8. Click the **Routing and Remote Access** node to select it. Click **Action** on the menu bar and then click **Configure and Enable Routing and Remote Access** to start the Routing and Remote Access Server Setup Wizard.
9. Click **Next** in the first RRAS Setup Wizard window.
10. Click **Custom configuration** and then click **Next**.
11. In the Custom Configuration window, click **VPN access**, **Demand-dial connections**, **NAT**, and **LAN routing**, as shown in Figure 9-1, and then click **Next**. If a message appears regarding a default connection request policy, click **OK**.
12. Click **Finish** to close the wizard. In the message window, click **Start service** to start the RRAS service.
13. If necessary, click to expand the **Routing and Remote Access** node.
14. In the RRAS console, verify that the console icon includes a green arrow, as shown in Figure 9-2.
15. Right-click the **Ports** node and click **Properties** on the shortcut menu. The Ports Properties dialog box opens.
16. Click **WAN Miniport (PPTP)** and click **Configure**. Change the Maximum ports value to **1** and click **OK**.
17. When you receive a warning about reducing the number of ports, read the warning and click **Yes**.

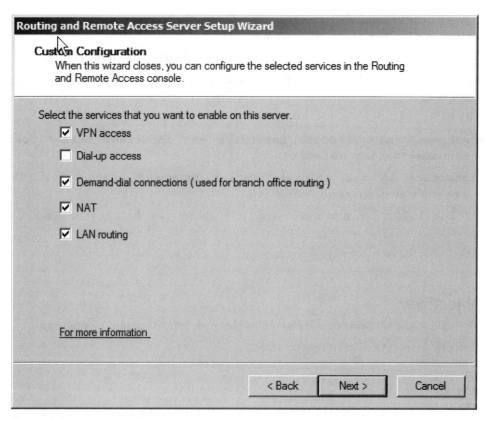

Figure 9-1 Custom Configuration window in the RRAS Setup Wizard

18. Click **WAN Miniport (L2TP)** and click **Configure**. Remove the check mark from the **Demand-dial routing connections (inbound and outbound)** check box, change the Maximum ports value to **1**, and click **OK**. Click **Yes** to close the warning window.

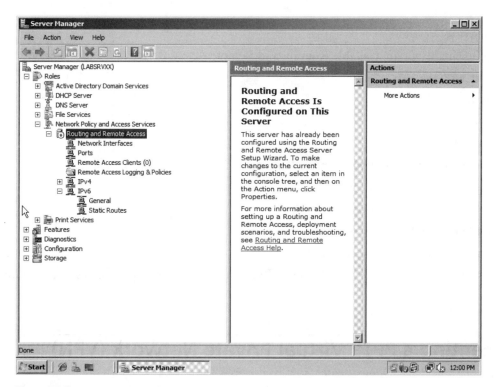

Figure 9-2 RRAS console after installation

19. Click **WAN Miniport (SSTP)** and click **Configure**. Change the Maximum ports value to **1** and click **OK**. Once again, click **Yes** to close the warning window.

20. Click **OK** to close the Ports Properties dialog box and apply the changes to the RRAS ports.

21. View the ports in the Ports pane, and you will notice the number of available ports has been reduced to one for each port type.

22. Log on to LABSRV1XX.

23. Open the command prompt and enter **netsh interface set interface name="local area connection" newname="Netlab Network"**.

24. Enter **netsh interface ip set address "Netlab Network" static 192.168.1.203 255.255.255.0** to set the IP address on LABSRV1XX.

25. Enter **ping 192.168.1.201**. You should receive a successful response back if your network is set up properly.

26. Leave both servers up for the next activity.

Certification Objectives

Objectives for MCTS Exam #70-642: Windows Server 2008 Network Infrastructure, Configuration:

- Configuring Network Access: Configure remote access

Review Questions

1. Which of the following steps are required for a default installation of Routing and Remote Access with PPTP and L2TP VPN connections? (Choose all that apply.)

   a. Install Routing and Remote Access role services

   b. Install a Network Policy Server

   c. Configure Routing and Remote Access

   d. Configure DNS to support RRAS

   e. Start the RRAS service

   f. Restart your server

2. Which of the following is not an available Routing and Remote Access device in Windows Server 2008?

   a. WAN Miniport (PPOE)

   b. WAN Miniport (PPTP)

   c. WAN Miniport (IPSEC)

   d. WAN Miniport (L2TP)

3. Which of the following can be configured in the Routing and Remote Access console?

   a. The IP addresses used by VPN clients

   b. The number of available VPN ports

   c. The Network Policy applied to users for remote access

   d. The users who can access a VPN connection

4. _____ is a type of VPN connection that uses IPSec and requires either certificates or pre-shared keys to implement.

Lab 9.2 Implementing a PPTP Virtual Private Network (VPN)

Objective

The objective of this activity is to configure user accounts and Windows clients with VPN remote access.

Materials Required

This lab requires the following:

- The LABSRVXX computer configured in previous activities
- The LABSRV1XX computer configured in the previous activity

Estimated completion time: **30 minutes**

Activity Background

Virtual Private Networks, or VPNs, are an excellent way to provide mobile or remote clients secure access to your network. Windows Server 2008 provides built-in VPN functionality through Routing and Remote Access. Once RRAS is configured for VPN access, users need to be given access in order to connect remotely. In this activity, you configure user access along with the VPN client on a remote computer.

Activity

1. Log on to LABSRVXX.

2. Open the command prompt. Enter **DSADD OU "OU=RRAS,DC=netlab,DC=local"** to create an organization unit called RRAS. Used in Active Directory environments, Dsadd is a command line utility for creating AD objects such as organizational units, users, and groups.

3. Open Active Directory Users and Computers and expand the nodes until you can highlight the **RRAS** OU.

4. From the Action menu, choose **New > User** to open the New Object - User window.

5. Enter the following information, as shown in Figure 9-3, and click **Next**.

   First Name: RRAS

   Last Name: One

   User logon name: rras1

6. Type **P@ssw0rd** in the Password and Confirm password text boxes, remove the check mark from the **User must change password at next logon** check box, and click **Next**.

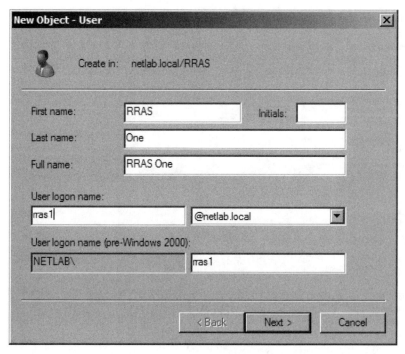

Figure 9-3   Creating a user object in Active Directory Users and Computers

7. Click **Finish** to complete the creation of the user.

8. Repeat the above steps to create a user object named RRAS2.

9. From the Action menu, choose **New > Group** to open the New Object - Group window.

10. Type **RRAS Users - GS** and click **OK** to create a global security group named RRAS Users - GS. This will be used in a later activity for assigning policies.

11. Click **RRAS Two** and then click **Add to a group** on the Action menu.

12. Type **RRAS Users - GS** in the text box of the Select Groups window, click **Check Names**, and click **OK**. This adds RRAS2 to the RRAS Users - GS group. Click **OK** in the confirmation box.

13. Leave Active Directory Users and Computers open and log on to LABSRV1XX.

14. Open the Control Panel and double-click **Network and Sharing Center**.

15. Click **Set up a connection or network** to launch the Set up a connection or network wizard.

16. Click **Connect to a workplace** and click **Next**.

17. Click **Use my Internet Connection (VPN)**.

18. Click **I'll set up an Internet connection later**.

19. Enter the IP address **192.168.1.201** in the Internet address text box and enter **RRAS VPN** in the Destination name text box, as shown in Figure 9-4. Click **Next**.

20. Enter the following user account information and click **Next**.

    Username: rras1

    Password: P@ssw0rd

21. Click to place a check mark in the **Remember this password** check box and click **Create**. Click **Close** when the connection has been created.

22. In the Network and Sharing Center window, click **Manage network connections**.

23. Click the RRAS VPN icon, click **Start this connection** on the toolbar, and click **Connect** to establish the VPN connection.

24. After a few seconds, you will see an error message appear. This is because the default Remote Access policy for all users is set to deny, so the user's account must be modified before being able to use the VPN.

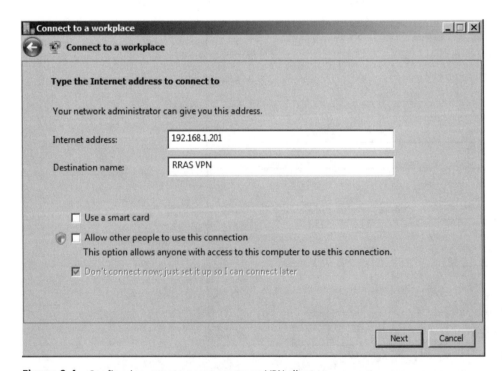

Figure 9-4   Configuring remote access server on VPN client

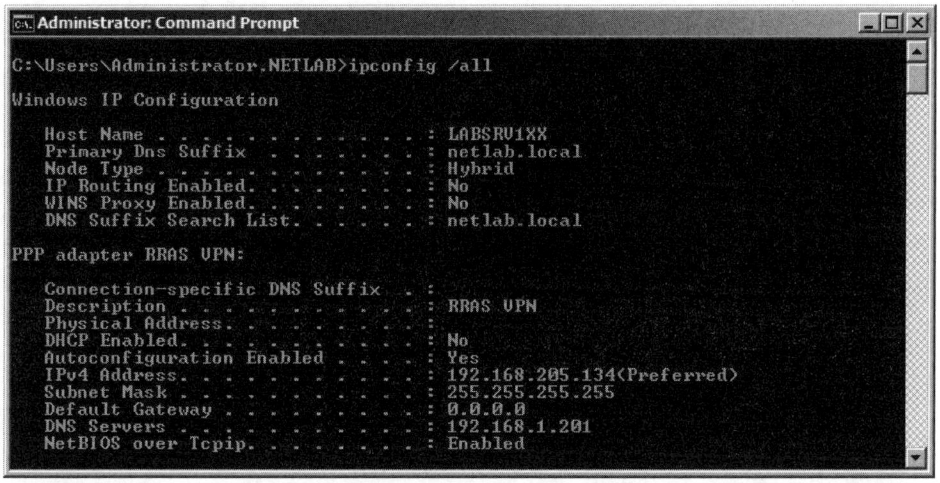

Figure 9-5 Results of ipconfig /all showing VPN IP information

25. Click **Close** in the error message window and switch back to LABSRVXX.

26. Open ADUC (if necessary), right-click **RRAS One**, and click **Properties**. On the Dial-in tab, click **Allow access** in the Network Access Permission section and click **OK** to close the properties window.

27. Switch back to LABSRV1XX and, with the RRAS VPN icon selected, click **Start this connection** on the toolbar, and then click **Connect**. This time the connection authenticates and you see the RRAS VPN connection connecting using WAN Miniport (PPTP). PPTP is used by default even if L2TP is configured on the Remote Access server.

28. Open the command prompt and enter **ipconfig /all** to view the PPP adapter RRAS VPN connection's IP configuration, similar to Figure 9-5.

29. Switch back to LABSRVXX and click the **Remote Access Clients** node in the Routing and Remote Access console. You should see a single connection listed.

30. Switch back to LABSRV1XX and disconnect the RRAS VPN Connection. Leave both servers on for the next activity.

Certification Objectives

Objectives for MCTS Exam #70-642: Windows Server 2008 Network Infrastructure, Configuration:

- Configuring Network Access: Configure remote access

Review Questions

1. You have just implemented Remote Access VPN connections using PPTP for your remote users. No changes have been made to Routing and Remote Access, so it is running with default settings. Due to time constraints, you did not implement a Network Policy Server or establish a Network Policy for remote access. All of the users have been configured with the same local VPN client settings; they are running Windows Vista Enterprise. Twenty out of the 25 users are able to connect. Which of the following is most likely the problem with the configuration?

   a. Users were not added to the Remote Users group.

   b. The users' Dial-in properties need to be configured to allow remote access.

   c. The users' accounts need Log on locally rights to the Remote Access server.

   d. PPTP ports need to be modified to allow 25 connections instead of the default.

2. Given a default user account in Windows Server 2008, which of the following steps will provide a user remote access using a PPTP VPN connection? (Choose all that apply.)

   a. Install Routing and Remote Access role services

   b. Configure Routing and Remote Access

    c. Configure the PPTP port to use a pre-shared key

    d. Change user Dial-in properties to allow remote access

    e. Add the user to the Remote Users group in Active Directory

    f. Configure the client VPN connection using the IP address of the Remote Access server

    g. Install pre-shared key on client computer

3. Which of the following can be configured in Active Directory Users and Computers? (Choose all that apply.)

    a. The IP addresses used by VPN clients

    b. The number of available VPN ports

    c. The Network Policy applied to users for remote access

    d. The users who can access a VPN connection

4. _____ is used to configure a domain user's dial-in properties.

5. True or False? The default Network Access permission on the Dial-in tab for a user object is set to Deny access.

Lab 9.3 Configuring a Network Policy for Remote Access Users

Objective

The objective of this activity is to configure network policies for remote access clients.

Materials Required

This lab requires the following:

- The LABSRVXX computer configured in previous activities
- The LABSRV1XX computer configured in previous activities

> Estimated completion time: **30 minutes**

Activity Background

The Network Policy Server in Windows Server 2008 allows administrators to manage RADIUS, Network Access Protection, and policies. With NPS, you can configure a central network policy for handling remote access client requests, including which users or groups can connect and how they can connect. In this activity, you will work with policies related to remote access.

Activity

1. Log on to LABSRVXX.

2. Open Server Manager and click **Network Policy and Access Services**.

3. In the summary pane, scroll down until you see the installed role services. Click **Add Role Services** to begin the installation process for the Network Policy Server role service.

4. In the Select Role Services window, place a check mark in the **Network Policy Server** check box, click **Next,** and then click **Install**. Wait a few minutes for the installation to complete, and then click **Close.**

5. Click **Start**, point to **Administrative Tools**, and click **Network Policy Server (NPS)**.

6. In the NPS console, expand **Policies** and click **Network Policies**.

7. Click **Action** on the menu bar and click **New** to open the New Network Policy wizard. This wizard allows you to create a new Remote Access policy.

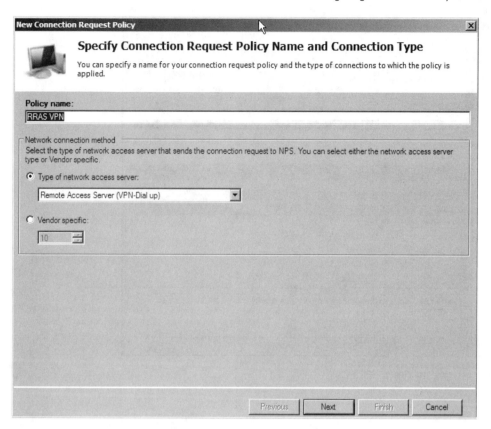

Figure 9-6 Configuring network policy in the Network Policy Server console

8. Type **RRAS VPN** as the policy name and choose **Remote Access Server (VPN-Dial up)** as the type of network access server, as shown in Figure 9-6. Click **Next**.

9. In the Specify Conditions window, click **Add**, click **User Groups** on the condition list, and then click **Add**.

10. Click **Add** Groups, type **RRAS Users - GS** as the Group name and click **OK** twice. Click **Next** twice.

11. Click **Next** to accept the default authentication methods.

12. Place a check mark in the **Disconnect after the maximum idle time** check box next to the Idle Timeout constraint and leave the default of 1 minute. This configures the VPN connection to disconnect after being Idle for one minute. Click **Next**.

13. Under Settings, click **IP Settings** and change the settings to **Assign a static IPv4 address**. Type **192.168.1.210** as the static IP address and click **Next**.

14. Review the policy settings and click **Finish**. This creates the new network policy and makes it available for use by members of the RRAS User - GS global security group.

15. In the list of policies, verify that **RRAS VPN** is listed with the top processing order of "3" as shown in Figure 9-7.

16. Right-click **Connections to Microsoft Routing and Remote Access server** and choose disable from the Action menu.

17. Close the NPS console.

18. Log on to LABSRV1XX.

19. Navigate back to the Network Connections window (if necessary), click **RRAS VPN**, and click **Start this connection** on the toolbar. Type **RRAS2** as the user Name and **P@ssw0rd** as the password, and click **Connect**. The connection authenticates and you see the RRAS VPN connection connected using WAN Miniport (PPTP).

20. Open a command prompt and type **ipconfig /all**. Review the output and verify that the PPP connection has an IP address of 192.168.1.210 listed.

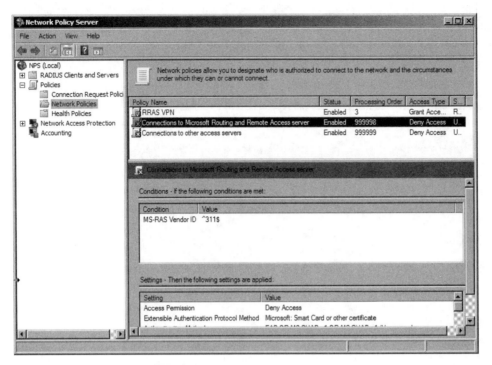

Figure 9-7   Available network policies in NPS

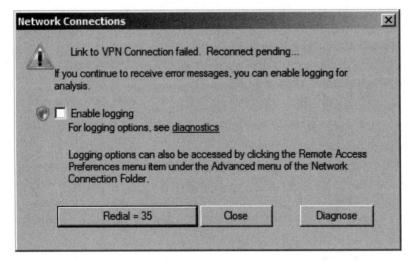

Figure 9-8   Idle time-out error on VPN client

21. Once the VPN is connected, let LABSRV1XX sit idle for approximately one minute. After about a minute, you will receive a connection error similar to Figure 9-8. This is due to the idle timeout set by the RRAS VPN policy. Click **Close** to remain disconnected.

22. Log off LABSRV1XX.

Certification Objectives

Objectives for MCTS Exam #70-642: Windows Server 2008 Network Infrastructure, Configuration:

- Configuring Network Access: Configure remote access

Review Questions

1. Which role service is required to create a Network Policy for Remote Access?

   a. Network Access Protection

   b. Routing

   c. Remote Access

   d. Network Policy Server

2. Which role service is required by Windows Server 2008 to provide VPN client access to a network?

   a. Network Access Protection

   b. Routing

   c. Remote Access

   d. Network Policy Server

3. Which of the following can be used to configure a static IP address for VPN clients? (Choose all that apply.)

   a. Network Policy Server

   b. Routing and Remote Access

   c. Active Directory Users and Computers

   d. Network Connections

   e. Netsh

4. Network policies that have higher priority should be moved _____ in the processing order.

5. True or False? The default network policies installed in NPS allow users remote access.

MANAGING SECURITY IN WINDOWS SERVER 2008

Labs included in this chapter

- Lab 10.1 Deploying Security Policies with Security Configuration Wizard

- Lab 10.2 Applying Firewall Rules through Group Policy

- Lab 10.3 Scanning Domain Computers with Microsoft Baseline Security Analyzer

- Lab 10.4 Establishing an L2TP VPN Using Preshared Keys

Microsoft MCTS Exam #70-642 Objectives

Objective	Lab
Configuring Network Access: Configure firewall settings	10.1, 10.2
Configure Network Access: Configure network authentication	10.4

Lab 10.1 Deploying Security Policies with Security Configuration Wizard

Objectives

The objective of this activity is to configure a server security policy and install the policy on another computer.

Materials Required

This lab requires the following:

- The LABSRVXX computer configured in previous activities
- The LABSRV1XX computer configured in previous activities

Estimated completion time: **30 minutes**

Activity Background

First introduced in Windows Server 2003 SP2, the Security Configuration Wizard is a utility for configuring security settings with the need for multiple consoles. It provides the ability to create, edit, apply, and rollback security policies on a Windows Server 2008 computer.

Activity

1. Log on to LABSRV1XX as Administrator.

2. Open the command prompt and enter **netsh int ipv4 set dns "Netlab Network" static 192.168.1.201**. This configures LABSRV1XX to use LABSRVXX (192.168.1.201) as its DNS server.

3. Enter **netdom join LABSRV1XX /domain:netlab.local /userd:administrator /passwordd:P@ssw0rd** to join LABSRV1XX to the netlab.local domain.

4. Enter **shutdown /r /t 0** to restart LABSRV1XX.

5. After LABSRV1XX restarts, log on as **administrator@netlab.local** with a password of **P@ssw0rd**.

6. Open the command prompt and enter **md c:\SCWpolicies**.

7. Enter **net share SCWPolicies=c:\SCWPolicies /Grant:Everyone,Change** to create a shared folder called SCWPolicies where the Everyone group has the ability to change the folder contents. This will be used to store the security policy created in this activity on LABSRV1XX.

8. Log onto LABSRVXX as administrator.

9. Open the command prompt and enter **net use x: \\labsrv1xx\scwpolicies** to create a mapped network drive to LABSRV1XX.

10. From the Start menu, open Administrative Tools, and then start the Security Configuration Wizard.

11. Click **Next** on the Welcome screen.

12. Click **Next** in the Configuration Action window to accept the default option of **Create a new security policy**.

13. On the Select Server window, enter **LABSRV1XX** as the base server and click **Next**. This specifies the member server, LABSRV1XX, as the base for creating a new security policy.

14. Click **View Configuration Database** to open the SCW Viewer. If you receive an ActiveX control warning, click **Yes**.

15. After reviewing the settings, close the SCW Viewer and then click **Next**.

16. Click **Next** in the Role-Based Service Configuration window.

17. In the Select Server Roles window, click **Next** to accept the default selection of installed roles.

18. In the Select Client Features window, click **Next** to accept the default selection of installed features.

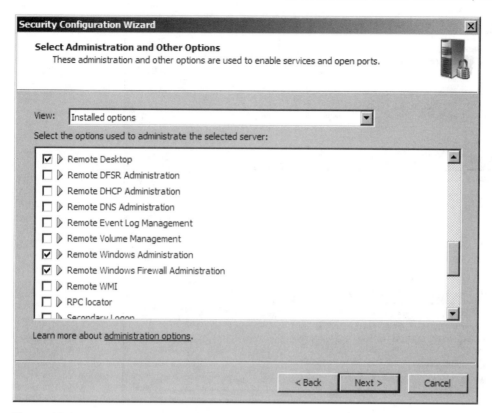

Figure 10-1   Selecting options settings in Security Configuration Wizard

19. In the Select Administration and Other Options window, browse and select **Remote Desktop, Remote Windows Administration,** and **Remote Windows Firewall Administration** to add each option to the existing list of options, as shown in Figure 10-1. Click **Next**.

20. In the Select Additional Services window, click **Next**.

21. In the Handling Unspecified Services window, click **Next** to accept the default selection.

22. Review the list of changed services and then click **Next**.

23. In the Network Security window, click the **Skip this section** check box and then click **Next**.

24. In the Registry Settings window, click the **Skip this section** check box and then click **Next**.

25. In the Audit Policy window, click the **Skip this section** check box and then click **Next**.

26. In the Save Security Policy window, click **Next**.

27. Type **x:\NewPolicy** as the security policy file name and type **This is a new security policy** as the description, as shown in Figure 10-2. Click **Next**. This saves the security policy as an xml file, the default file type, to LABSRV1XX.

28. In the Apply Security Policy window, click **Next** to accept the default of Apply later.

29. Click **Finish** to complete the SCW.

30. Log on to LABSRV1XX.

31. From the Start menu, open Administrative Tools, and then start the Security Configuration Wizard.

32. Click **Next** on the Welcome screen.

33. In the Configuration Action window, click **Apply an existing security policy**, type **c:\scwpolicies\newpolicy.xml** in the Existing security policy file text box, and click **Next**.

34. Click **Next** in the Select Server window to accept the default of LABSRV1XX.

35. Click **Next** in the Apply Security Policy window. Once the application of the policy is completed, click **Next** and **Finish**.

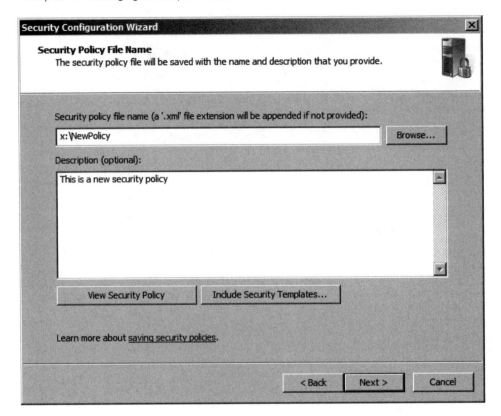

Figure 10-2   Saving a custom security policy

Certification Objectives

Objectives for MCTS Exam #70-642: Windows Server 2008 Network Infrastructure, Configuration:

- Configuring Network Access: Configure remote access

Review Questions

1. Which of the following are not configured with the Security Configuration Wizard?

    a. Network Security

    b. Registry Settings

    c. Group Policy Settings

    d. Audit Policy

2. What is the default file format for policies created with the Security Configuration Wizard?

    a. .pol

    b. .xls

    c. .xml

    d. .csv

3. Which of the following is not a configuration action in the Security Configuration Wizard?

    a. Create a new security policy

    b. Create a new security policy using an existing security policy

    c. Edit an existing security policy

    d. Rollback the last applied security Policy

4. True or False? The Security Configuration Wizard must be installed through Add Features before it can be used in Windows Server 2008.

5. _____ allows an administrator to return a computer to the state prior to applying the most recent security policy.

Lab 10.2 Applying Firewall Rules through Group Policy

Objective

The objective of this activity is to create a Group Policy Object for deploying WFAS settings.

Materials Required

This lab requires the following:

- The LABSRVXX computer configured in previous activities
- The LABSRV1XX computer configured in previous activities

Estimated completion time: **30 minutes**

Activity Background

For networks using Active Directory Domain Services, Group Policy Objects (GPOs) are the most efficient way for deploying computer and user settings. The use of GPOs allows for the creation of a central policy for things like firewall exceptions. Once created, this GPO can be applied to multiple computer or user objects on the network. GPOs allow for two types of configuration settings: user and computer. As their names imply, user settings apply to user objects and computer settings apply to computer objects. For deploying a firewall rule, you will use computer settings when creating a GPO. Then you will apply this GPO to an organizational unit that contains the computer object that is to get the settings.

10

Activity

1. Log on to LABSRV1XX as Administrator.
2. Open the command prompt and enter **servermanagercmd.exe -install web-webserver**. Once the installation is complete, close the command prompt window.
3. Open **Internet Explorer** and enter **http://LABSRV1XX** in the Address bar to display the IIS 7 welcome page. If the Microsoft Phishing Filter window opens, click the **Turn off automatic Phishing Filter** option button, and then click **OK**. Close **Internet Explorer**.
4. Click **Start**, point to **Administrative Tools**, and then click **Windows Firewall with Advanced Security**.
5. Click **Inbound Rules** in the left pane and then double-click the **World Wide Web Services (HTTP Traffic-In)** firewall rule in the middle pane.
6. In the Properties dialog box, click the **Advanced** tab, select **These profiles** and **Private**, and click **OK**.
7. Click **Start**, type **http://localhost** in the Start Search box, and press **Enter** to open Internet Explorer. You will see the IIS7 default screen as shown in Figure 10-3. This verifies that a Web page is still available on LABSRV1XX after applying the firewall rule in Step 5.
8. From the Start menu, open Administrative Tools, and then start the Security Configuration Wizard.
9. Click **Next** on the Welcome screen.
10. In the Configuration Action window, click **Rollback the last applied security policy** and click **Next** three times to begin the rollback of the security policy applied in the last activity.
11. Once completed, click **Next** and **Finish**.
12. Log off LABSRV1XX.
13. Log on to LABSRVXX.
14. Open the command prompt and enter **dsadd OU "OU=Servers,dc=netlab,dc=local"**. This command creates an organizational unit to be used for applying group policy to member servers.
15. Enter **dsmove "CN=LABSRV1XX,CN=Computers,DC=netlab,DC=local" -newparent "OU=Servers, dc=netlab,dc=local"** to move LABSRV1XX into the Server organizational unit.

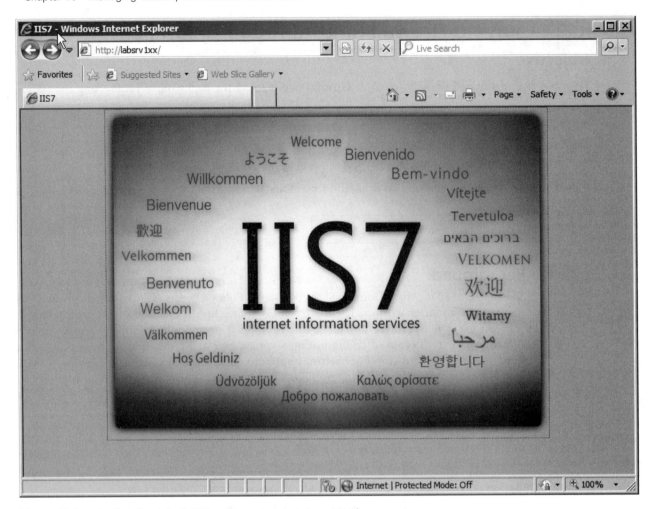

Figure 10-3 Viewing the default IIS7 welcome page in Internet Explorer

16. Click **Start**, type **http://labsrv1xx** in the Start Search box, and press **Enter** to open Internet Explorer. This will fail because the firewall was modified earlier. Close Internet Explorer.

17. On the Start menu, point to **Administrative Tools**, and then click **Group Policy Management**. This launches the Group Policy Management Console, the tool necessary for creating Group Policy Objects.

18. Expand the Group Policy Management nodes until Servers is highlighted.

19. On the Action menu, click **Create a GPO in this domain, and Link it here**.

20. In the New GPO dialog box, enter **FirewallPolComp** as the name of the new group policy object and click **OK**. This creates a new link for a GPO, as shown in Figure 10-4.

21. Expand the **Servers** node, if necessary, Highlight **FirewallPolComp**, and click **Edit** on the Action menu. If the Group Policy Management Console message box appears, click **OK** and repeat this step.

22. In the Group Policy Management Editor, Expand **Computer Configuration > Policies > Administrative Templates > Network > Network Connections >Windows Firewall**, and then click **Domain Profile**, as shown in Figure 10-5. The Group Policy Management Editor is used to configure the individual computer and user settings within a Group Policy Object.

23. In the right pane, double-click **Windows Firewall: Define inbound port exceptions**, click **Enabled** and click **Show**.

24. Click **Add**, type **80:TCP:*:enabled:Web Service,** then click **OK** three times to add the new setting.

25. Close the Group Policy Management Editor and Group Policy Management Console.

26. Switch back to LABSRV1XX, open the command prompt, and enter **gpupdate /force** to ensure the newly-created GPO is applied to LABSRV1XX.

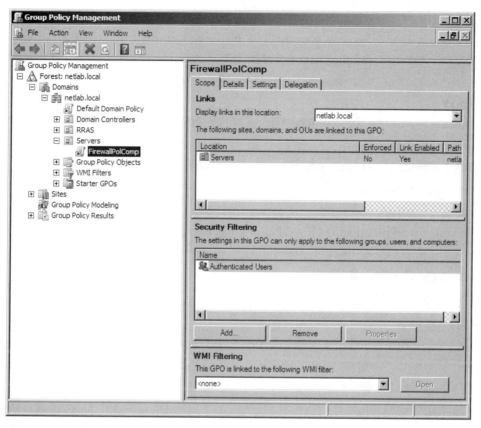

Figure 10-4 New Group Policy Object linked in Group Policy Management Console

27. Once completed, close the command prompt and switch back to LABSRVXX.

28. Click **Start**, type **http://labsrv1xx**, and press **Enter** to open Internet Explorer. This opens the default start page, since the rule you created above overrides the local firewall settings.

29. Close **Internet Explorer**.

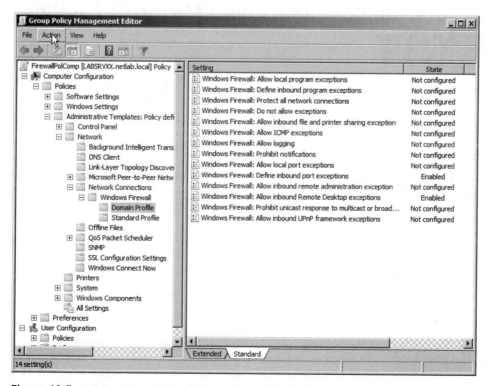

Figure 10-5 Editing Group Policy Object settings with the Group Policy Object Editor

Certification Objectives

Objectives for MCTS Exam #70-642: Windows Server 2008 Network Infrastructure, Configuration:

- Configuring Network Access: Configure remote access

Review Questions

1. Which of the following is required for deploying Group Policy Objects to computer objects in a domain?

    a. Active Directory Federated Services

    b. Active Directory Light-Weight Directory Services

    c. Active Directory Domain Services

    d. Active Directory Certificate Services

2. Which of the following is used for creating Group Policy Objects and applying them to organizational units?

    a. Active Directory Users and Computers

    b. Group Policy Management Console

    c. Group Policy Management Editor

    d. Server Manager

3. Which of the following is used for adding computer configuration settings to a Group Policy Object?

    a. Active Directory Users and Computers

    b. Group Policy Management Console

    c. Group Policy Management Editor

    d. Server Manager

4. _____ can be run on client computers to initiate an update of Group Policy.

5. True or False? Because they are explicitly assigned to a machine, local firewall settings cannot be overridden by firewall settings delivered through Group Policy.

Lab 10.3 Scanning Domain Computers with Microsoft Baseline Security Analyzer

Objectives

The objective of this activity is to scan multiple domain computers with MBSA.

Materials Required

This lab requires the following:

- The LABSRVXX computer configured in previous activities. An Internet connection.
- The LABSRV1XX computer configured in previous activities.
- This lab requires the current edition of Microsoft Baseline Security Analyzer. MBSA is available as a free download from **www.microsoft.com**.

Estimated completion time: **30 minutes**

Activity Background

Microsoft Baseline Security Analyzer (MBSA) is an excellent tool for performing an initial analysis of your current security setup. The MBSA can scan single or multiple computers on a network or view existing security scan reports. The reports generated by MBSA include information such as missing Windows updates and local account security settings.

Activity

1. Log on to LABSRV1XX as Administrator.

2. Open the command prompt and enter **netsh firewall set service fileandprint**.

3. Log onto LABSRVXX as administrator.

4. Download the current edition of Microsoft Baseline Security Analyzer from www.microsoft.com, or ask your instructor where to acquire the setup file. Save the setup file to c:\MBSAsetup on LABSRVXX.

The version of MBSA used at the time of writing is 2.1.1.

5. Browse to c:\MBSAsetup and double-click the setup file for MBSA. Click **Next** to begin Setup.

6. On the License agreement screen, choose **I accept the license agreement**, click **Next** two times, and click **Install**. When the installation is complete, click **OK**.

7. Click **Start**, click **All Programs**, and click **Microsoft Baseline Security Analyzer 2.1**.

8. Click **Scan multiple computers** and type **netlab** as the domain name, as shown in Figure 10-6.

9. Click **Start Scan**. The scan takes a couple of minutes to complete, and you receive a message that LABSCXX was unable to be scanned, since it is not available at this time.

10. Click **Pick a security report to view**. You see a report for LABSRVXX and LABSRV1XX, as shown in Figure 10-7.

11. Click **Netlab\LABSRVXX** to view the MBSA report for the local system.

12. Under Security Update Scan Results, click **Result details** for Windows Security Updates. This provides a listing of all missing Windows updates along with descriptions of each update and the ability to download individual updates from Microsoft. Close the Windows Security Updates window.

13. Scroll to the bottom of the report and click **Next security report** to view the report for LABSRV1XX.

14. Review the report and click **OK** when completed. The report for LABSRV1XX may list an incomplete scan due to Windows Update on LABSRV1XX.

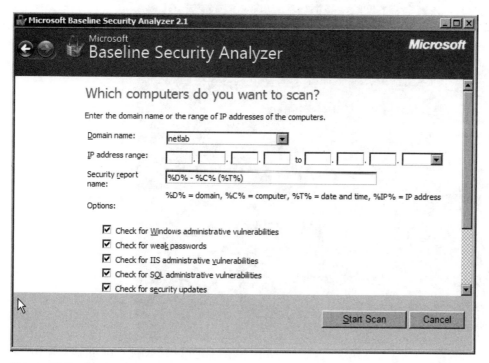

Figure 10-6 Scanning multiple computers with MBSA

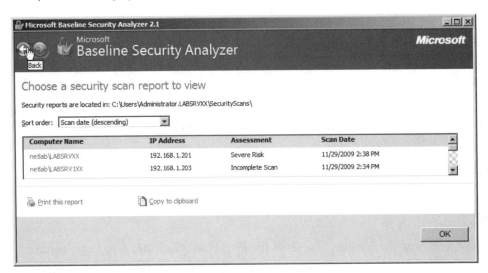

Figure 10-7 Available security reports in MBSA

15. Open a command prompt and enter **cd c:\Program Files\Microsoft Baseline Security Analyzer 2**.

16. Enter **mbsacli.exe /?** to view the usage and syntax for the mbsacli.exe command.

17. Enter **mbsacli.exe /target LABSRVXX /n SQL**. This runs MBSA from the command line using mbsacli.exe. It targets LABSRVXX and excludes checks for SQL vulnerabilities. Mbsacli.exe can be used just like the GUI tool for scanning single or multiple computers.

18. Review the results of the scan in the command prompt window, as shown in Figure 10-8. Also, reports generated from the command line can be viewed through the GUI MBSA tool.

19. Close all open windows.

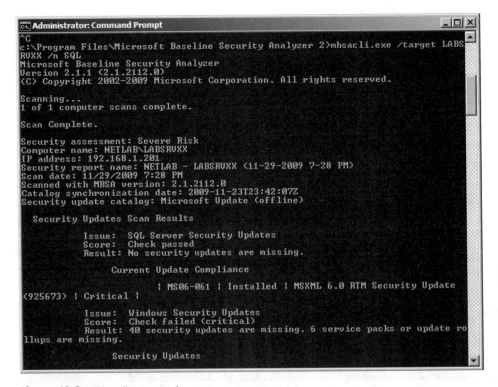

Figure 10-8 Mbsacli scan results

Review Questions

1. Which of the following commands will perform an MBSA scan of operating system updates, SQL vulnerabilities, and password settings on the remote computer 192.168.1.201?

   a. mbsacli.exe /d 192.168.1.201 /n IIS

   b. mbsacli.exe /t 192.168.1.201 /n

   c. mbsacli.exe /Target 192.168.1.201

   d. mbsacli.exe /Target 192.168.1.201/n IIS

2. Which of the following items are not included in an MBSA scan report? Include all that apply.

   a. Updates for Microsoft products

   b. Updates for third-party products

   c. The number of accounts with expiring passwords

   d. Microsoft Exchange vulnerabilities

   e. The names of accounts with administrative permissions

3. Which switch is used with mbsacli.exe to specify items to skip in an MBSA scan?

   a. /d

   b. /s

   c. /n

   d. /t

4. True or False? The Microsoft Baseline Security Analyzer is available as a Feature in Windows Server 2008.

5. Links for running the Microsoft Baseline Security Analyzer are available from the Start menu and a computer's _____.

10

Lab 10.4 Establishing an L2TP VPN Using Preshared Keys

Objective

The objective of this activity is to configure an IPSec L2TP VPN using preshared keys.

Materials Required

This lab requires the following:

- The LABSRVXX computer configured in previous activities
- The LABSRV1XX computer configured in previous activities

Estimated completion time: **30 minutes**

Activity Background

Internet Protocol Security, or IPSec, is an open-standards framework for securing network communications. Its uses include server-to-server communication and virtual private network (VPN) communication. In Windows Server 2008, IPSec-secured remote access solutions use Layer 2 Tunneling Protocol (L2TP) for implementing VPN connections. IPSec can use different authentication methods including preshared keys. This form of authentication uses a string of characters, known as the preshared key, that is provided to all IPSec peers participating in the communications. Every peer that participates in the same security policy will need the same preshared key. Shared secrets don't remain secret for very long. Furthermore, they're stored in the registry and are clearly visible to anyone with administrative privileges on the computer.

Activity

1. Log on to LABSRVXX as Administrator.

2. Open Routing and Remote Access from the Administrative Tools menu.

3. In the RRAS console, click **LABSRVXX (local)** and click **Properties** on the Action menu.

4. Click the **Security** tab and choose **Allow custom IPSec policy for L2TP connection**.

5. In the Preshared Key text box, enter **L2TPpassword** as the key, as shown in Figure 10-9, and click **OK** twice. This allows you to establish an L2TP connection using a preshared key.

6. Log on to LABSRV1XX and open the **Network and Sharing Center** from Control Panel.

7. Click **Set up a connection or network** to launch the Set up a connection or network wizard.

8. Click **Connect to a workplace** and click **Next**.

9. Click **Use my Internet Connection (VPN)**.

10. Click **I'll set up an Internet connection later**.

11. Enter the IP address **labsrvxx.netlab.local** and a destination name of **L2TP VPN**, and then click **Next**.

12. Enter the following user account information, choose **Remember this password**, and click **Next**.

    Username: rras2

    Password: P@ssw0rd

13. Click **Create** and then click **Close** to close the Connect to a workplace wizard.

14. In Network and Sharing Center, click **Manage network connections**.

15. Right-click the **L2TP VPN** icon and click **Properties** on the shortcut menu.

16. On the Networking tab, choose **L2TP IPSec VPN** from the dropdown menu for VPN type and click **IPsec Settings**.

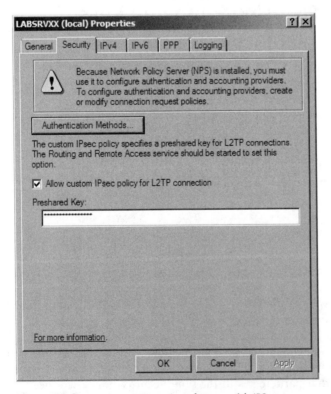

Figure 10-9   Setting L2TP settings for use with IPSec

```
Administrator: Command Prompt                                        _ □ ×

C:\Users\Administrator.NETLAB>ipconfig /all

Windows IP Configuration

    Host Name . . . . . . . . . . . . : LABSRV1XX
    Primary Dns Suffix  . . . . . . . : netlab.local
    Node Type . . . . . . . . . . . . : Hybrid
    IP Routing Enabled. . . . . . . . : No
    WINS Proxy Enabled. . . . . . . . : No
    DNS Suffix Search List. . . . . . : netlab.local

PPP adapter L2TP Connection:

    Connection-specific DNS Suffix  . :
    Description . . . . . . . . . . . : L2TP Connection
    Physical Address. . . . . . . . . :
    DHCP Enabled. . . . . . . . . . . : No
    Autoconfiguration Enabled . . . . : Yes
    IPv4 Address. . . . . . . . . . . : 192.168.1.210(Preferred)
    Subnet Mask . . . . . . . . . . . : 255.255.255.255
    Default Gateway . . . . . . . . . : 0.0.0.0
    DNS Servers . . . . . . . . . . . : 192.168.1.201
    NetBIOS over Tcpip. . . . . . . . : Enabled
```

Figure 10-10   Setting L2TP settings for use with IPSec

17. Click **Use preshared key for authentication** and enter **L2TPpassword** as the key. Click **OK**, and then click **OK** again to close the L2TP VPN Properties dialog box. Click the **L2TP VPN** icon and click **Start this connection** on the toolbar. Click **Connect** to establish the VPN connection.

18. Open the command prompt and type **ipconfig /all**. You see an entry for the **PPP adapter L2TP VPN** using the IP address of 192.168.1.205, as shown in Figure 10-10.

19. Close all open windows and log off LABSRV1XX.

Certification Objectives

Objectives for MCTS Exam #70-642: Windows Server 2008 Network Infrastructure, Configuration:

- Configuring Network Access: Configure remote access

Review Questions

1. Which of the following property tabs is used to configure a preshared key on the client VPN connection?

   a. General

   b. Networking

   c. Advanced

   d. Security

2. Which of the following authentication methods is not available for use with IPSec?

   a. Kerberos V.5

   b. Digital Certificates

   c. RADIUS

   d. Preshared key

3. Which of the following port types can be used for VPN access? (Choose all that apply).

   a. WAN Miniport (PPOE)

   b. WAN Miniport (PPTP)

   c. WAN Miniport (L2TP)

   d. WAN Miniport (SSTP)

4. True or False? Using preshared keys requires configuration on the Remote Access server only.

5. L2TP is short for _____.

CHAPTER ELEVEN

MANAGING AND MONITORING A WINDOWS SERVER 2008 INFRASTRUCTURE

Labs included in this chapter

- Lab 11.1 Backing Up Windows Server 2008 to a Network Location
- Lab 11.2 Restoring Windows Server 2008 Using WinRE and Network Backup
- Lab 11.3 Creating a Backup Scheme for a Network

Microsoft MCTS Exam #70-642 Objectives

Objective	Lab
Configure File and Print Services: Configure backup and restore	11.1, 11.2, 11.3

Lab 11.1 Backing Up Windows Server 2008 to a Network Location

Objectives

The objective of this lab is to practice backing up a Windows Server 2008 server to a remote location.

Materials Required

This lab requires the following:

- The LABSRVXX computer configured in previous activities. This machine will require at least 20GB of free space to perform backup activities.
- The LABSRV1XX computer configured in previous activities.

Estimated completion time: **60–90 minutes**

Activity Background

Windows Server Backup (WSB) is the built-in backup utility for Windows Server 2008. In addition to allowing administrators to perform a backup to a local or external hard disk, WSB supports full server backups to a remote file share. This is an excellent way to centrally store all system backups for possible offsite backup. In this activity, you will practice installing and using Windows Server Backup.

Activity

1. Log on to LABSRVXX as administrator.

2. Open the Computer Management snap-in and, in the left pane, click **Disk Management** under Storage.

3. Click the **C:** volume, if necessary. On the Action menu, point to **All Tasks > Extend Volume** from the Action menu. This launches the Extend Volume Wizard. If you do not have the option to extend the volume, delete any existing disk volumes except for C: and retry the step above. Click **Next** on the Welcome to the Extend Volume Wizard page.

4. Accept the default amount of space on the **Select Disks** page, as shown in Figure 11-1, by clicking **Next**. The amount of space available for extending the volume may differ from the figure based on your lab environment and computer setup. On the Completing the Extend Volume Wizard page, click **Finish**.

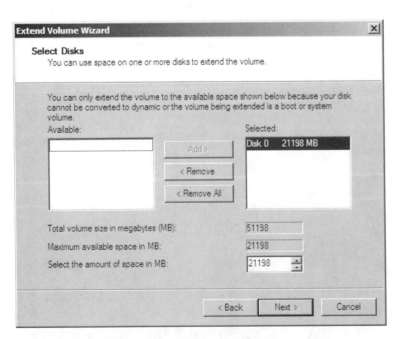

Figure 11-1 Extending a disk volume

5. In Disk Management, verify that the C: volume has expanded by the amount of space added in Step 4 and then close the **Computer Management** console.

6. Open a command prompt and enter **md "c:\Chapter 11\RemoteBackups"** to create a folder for storing remote Windows Server backups.

7. Enter **net share RemoteBackups="c:\Chapter 11\RemoteBackups" /Grant:Everyone,Change** to create a shared folder for backups.

8. Enter **servermanagercmd -i Backup-Features Backup-Tools** to install the Windows Server Backup features and command-line tools on LABSRVXX. Once the installation process is completed, close the command prompt window.

9. Log on to LABSRV1XX.

10. Open a command prompt and enter **servermanagercmd -i Backup-Features Backup-Tools** to install the Windows Server Backup features and command-line tools.

11. Click **Windows Server Backup** on the Administrative Tools menu.

12. In the Windows Server Backup Console, click **Backup Once** to configure a one-time backup, and then click **Next** on the first page of the Backup Once Wizard.

13. On the Select backup configuration page, review the approximate backup size. Before proceeding, verify you have enough space on LABSRVXX to store the backup being created. Click **Next** to proceed with configuration of the backup.

14. Click **Remote shared folder** and click **Next**.

15. Type **\\LABSRVXX\RemoteBackups** as shown in Figure 11-2 to configure the backup to be stored on LABSRVXX. Click **Next** to continue.

16. Review each of the VSS backup options. After reviewing each item, choose **VSS full backup** and click **Next**.

17. Review the confirmation page and click **Backup** to proceed. Depending on your lab environment, the backup time will vary. When the backup has completed, click **Close**.

18. Switch to LABSRVXX and browse to **c:\Chapter 11\Remote Backups\WindowsImageBackup** using Windows Explorer. There will be a folder labeled LABSRV1XX. This folder contains all of the backup and catalog files created by the backup job.

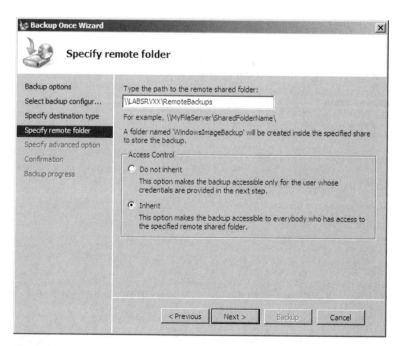

Figure 11-2 Configuring backup to use a remote shared folder

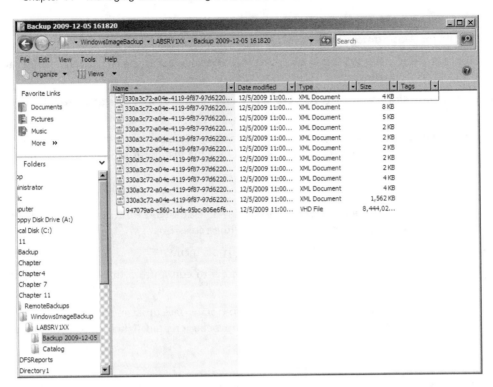

Figure 11-3   Windows Server Backup files in Windows Explorer

19. Double-click the **LABSRV1XX** folder and then double-click the folder beginning with **Backup**. As shown in Figure 11-3, this displays the backup files, including the .vhd file that contains the backup image.

20. Close all open windows and log off LABSRVXX.

Certification Objectives

Objectives for MCTS Exam #70-642: Windows Server 2008 Network Infrastructure, Configuration:

- Configure File and Print Services: Configure backup and restore

Review Questions

1. Which of the following VSS backup types is used when you are not using another backup product and you wish for application logs to be deleted after the backup completes?

   a. VSS Incremental Backup

   b. VSS Copy Backup

   c. VSS Full Backup

   d. VSS Differential Backup

2. Windows Server Backup stores backups as the following file type:

   a. .bkf

   b. .vhd

   c. .zip

   d. .vmhd

3. Which of the following is a required component when installing the command-line tools for Windows Server Backup?

   a. .NET Framework 3.0

   b. Remote Server Administration Tools (RSAT)

    c. Windows PowerShell

    d. Removable Storage Manager

  4. True or False? The Windows Server Backup console allows you to create a backup schedule that uses a remote shared folder.

  5. _____ is the command line utility for Windows Server Backup.

Lab 11.2 Restoring Server 2008 Using WinRE and Network Backup

Objectives

The objective of this lab is to use Windows Recovery Environment to restore a Windows Server 2008 backup from a remote location.

Materials Required

This lab requires the following:

- The LABSRVXX computer configured in previous activities
- The LABSRV1XX computer configured in previous activities

Estimated completion time: **60–90 minutes**

Activity Background

With Windows Server Backup and Windows Recovery Environment (WinRE), administrators have a built-in solution for bare-metal, or full-server, restore of Windows Server 2008 computers. WinRE can be run from the Windows Server 2008 installation media or from the computer's hard drive, and it allows administrators to restore from local drives, external drives (such as USB portable drives), or from shared network locations. This provides a variety of options for restoring after a server failure.

Activity

1. Insert the Windows Server 2008 installation DVD into the DVD drive of LABSRV1XX and restart the computer. Make sure that your computer is configured to boot from the CD/DVD drive before the primary hard drive; select this option in the BIOS setup program, if necessary.

2. Press the space bar when **Press any key to boot from CD or DVD** appears. If necessary, press **Enter** to choose **Windows Setup** on the Windows Boot Manager screen.

3. Click **Next** at the **Install Windows** screen, and then click the **Repair your computer** link in the lower left-hand corner of the window.

4. Click **Next** in the System Recovery Options window and click **Command Prompt**. In the command prompt window, enter **start /w wpeinit** to initialize Windows PE and load the network adapter drivers. This will take 1–2 minutes.

5. Enter **ipconfig /all** and verify you receive an IP address in the range between 192.168.1.1 – 192.168.1.254. If you do not receive an IP address, verify that DHCP is running and that the scopes created in Lab 4.3 are configured correctly.

6. Enter **ping 192.168.1.201** and wait for the four successful replies. When completed, close the command prompt.

7. Click **Windows Complete PC Restore**, as shown in Figure 11-4.

8. When you receive a warning that a valid backup could not be found, click **Cancel.**

9. Click **Next** to choose a different backup and click **Advanced.**

11

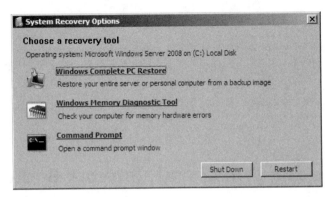

Figure 11-4   Available recovery tools from Windows Recovery Environment

10. Click **Search for a backup on the network** and click **Yes**.

11. Type **\\192.168.1.201\RemoteBackups** as the location of the backup, as shown in Figure 11-5, and click **OK**.

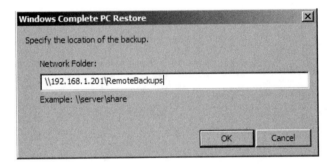

Figure 11-5   Specifying the location of the backup

12. When prompted for credentials, type **administrator@netlab.local** as the user name, type **P@ssw0rd** as the password, and then click **OK**.

13. Once authenticated, click the location of the backup you created in the previous activity and click **Next**.

14. Click the listed available backup for drive C: and click **Next**.

15. Click the **Format and repartition disks** check box and click **Next**. This causes the restore to format and repartition the computer's drive, which will erase the currently installed OS on LABSRV1XX.

16. Review the backup information and click **Finish** to begin the restoration process.

17. In the message box, click the **I confirm that I want to format the disks and restore the backup** check box, as shown in Figure 11-6, and click **OK**. The C: drive begins restoring the backup; depending on your lab computer, this process can take several minutes. Upon completion of the restore, the computer will reboot.

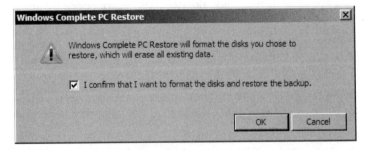

Figure 11-6   Windows Complete PC Restore confirmation dialog box

18. Log on to the restored LABSRV1XX.

19. In Server Manager, verify that the full computer name is LABSRV1XX.netlab.local.

20. Log off LABSRV1XX.

Certification Objectives

Objectives for MCTS Exam #70-642: Windows Server 2008 Network Infrastructure, Configuration:

- Configure File and Print Services: Configure backup and restore

Review Questions

1. Which of the following commands must be run before WinRE has access to its network adapters?

   a. start /w wpeinit

   b. start /w winreinit

   c. start /w wbadmin -Init

   d. start /w ntdsutil

2. Which of the following is not an option for accessing a backup set for restore when using WinRE?

   a. USB drive

   b. Remote network share via UNC path

   c. Remote network share via mapped drive

   d. Local drive volume

3. Which of the following provides access to Windows Complete PC Restore?

   a. Windows Server 2008 media

   b. Windows Server 2008 rescue disk

   c. Windows PE custom boot disk

   d. Advanced Boot Menu

4. True or False? By default, a target disk will be formatted and repartitioned when restoring through Windows Recovery Environment.

5. A(n) _____ address is required in order for the Windows Recovery Environment to communicate with other network clients.

Lab 11.3 Creating a Backup Scheme for a Network

Objectives

The objective of this activity is to develop a backup scheme for a network.

Materials Required

This lab requires the following:

- A pencil or pen, and paper

Estimated completion time: **30–45 minutes**

Activity Background

Badger Widgets, LLC is a small manufacturing company in Southern Wisconsin. They have a small Windows Server 2008 environment with a total of two domain controllers and three member servers. Currently, no backup scenario is implemented for Badger Widgets. You have been asked to implement a backup and recovery scenario for Badger Widgets using Windows Server Backup. Requirements for the project include the following:

1. All servers must perform a full backup nightly.

2. All servers must be fully recoverable from the previous evening's backups.

3. BWSRV05 will be used as a central storage for backups. It will use a removable external USB drive for storing all backups.

4. Offsite storage of backups is a requirement for Badger Widgets' backup and recovery scenario.

5. Member servers do not include any applications such as Microsoft Exchange or SQL Server that would require special backup and restore procedures.

Activity

1. Detail the backup scheme you would implement for the given scenario. You will need to include the following:
   - Backup target on each machine
   - Destination of backups
   - Backup scheduling, including time and frequency of backup

2. List the steps you would take to restore a failed domain controller, given a restore to the same hardware.

3. List the steps you would take to restore a failed member server, given a restore to different hardware.

4. List the steps to configure Windows Server Backup on each server.

Certification Objectives

Objectives for MCTS Exam #70-642: Windows Server 2008 Network Infrastructure, Configuration:
   - Configure File and Print Services: Configure backup and restore

Review Questions

1. Which of the following tools are used for performing backups with Windows Server Backup? (Choose all that apply.)
   a. Windows Server Backup
   b. ntbackup
   c. wbadmin
   d. vssadmin

2. What type of restore is used when restoring deleted Active Directory objects?
   a. Incremental
   b. Non-authoritative
   c. Authoritative
   d. Full

3. Which of the following steps are needed when creating a scheduled backup that is stored on a remote server? (Choose all that apply.)
   a. Run the Schedule a backup wizard in the WSB console
   b. Create a batch file that uses wbadmin to perform a backup job
   c. Choose Shared Folder as the backup destination in the WSB console
   d. Create a scheduled task to run wbadmin
   e. Install the Removable Storage Manager

4. True or False? Only wbadmin can be used to create scheduled backups whose target is a local disk volume.

5. A _____ restore is used to restore a failed domain controller.

Index